Study to Teach

This book takes a fresh look at the process of studying. For all those preparing to teach or involved in further professional development it will provide an essential, accessible and readable companion to their course. Theories of learning are integrated with practical strategies for approaching a topic. Each of the following areas are discussed:

- writing clearly
- referencing
- active reading
- making notes
- using the library
- presenting your work orally
- developing subject knowledge
- using information and communications technology
- continuing professional development.

The book explores the process of getting to know yourself as a learner and the nature of knowledge and understanding. The contributory disciplines and curriculum studies are explored and the acquisition of subject knowledge receives both theoretical and practical attention. A useful and comprehensive introduction to research identifies and demystifies aspects more relevant to the education student. Also considered are the key relationships established during work in school which are so important to success.

Each chapter is written by professional educators with a wide range of experience and expertise. New and existing research findings are illustrated with examples and case studies from successful learners. The book also draws upon the powerful emerging models of partnership between schools and universities in developing reflective practitioners through action research and lifelong learning. It reflects the move towards a more diverse framework for teacher education and continuing professional development.

Steve Herne, **John Jessel** and **Jenny Griffiths** are all lecturers at the Department of Educational Studies at Goldsmiths College, University of London.

Study to Teach

A guide to studying in teacher education

Edited by Steve Herne,
John Jessel and Jenny Griffiths

London and New York

First published 2000
by Routledge
11 New Fetter Lane, London EC4P 4EE

Simultaneously published in the USA and Canada
by Routledge
29 West 35th Street, New York, NY 10001

Routledge is an imprint of the Taylor & Francis Group

Typeset in Perpetua by Taylor & Francis Books Ltd

Printed and bound in Great Britain by Biddles Ltd,
Guildford and King's Lynn

British Library Cataloguing in Publication Data
A catalogue record for this book is available from the British Library

Library of Congress Cataloging-in-Publication Data
Study to teach : a guide to studying in teacher education /
edited by Steve Herne, John Jessel, and Jenny Griffiths.
p. cm.
Includes bibliographical references and index.
(alk. paper)
1. Teachers–Training of. 2. Teaching. 3. Learning. I. Herne, Steve.
II. Jessel, John. III. Griffiths, Jenny.
LB1707.S88 2000 99-34506
370'71–dc21 CIP

ISBN 0–415–19112–2

Dedicated to all our students, past, present and future.

Contents

Illustrations

Figures

Tables

Boxes

Vignettes

Contributors

Barbara Allebone Lecturer in Maths Education, Goldsmiths College, University of London

Diana Coben Head of Programme, Higher Degrees (Education), Goldsmiths College, University of London

Daniel John Davies Senior Lecturer in Primary Science and Technology Education, Bath Spa University College

Rosalyn George Lecturer in Education, Goldsmiths College, University of London

Jenny Griffiths Lecturer in Education, Goldsmiths College, University of London

Steve Herne Lecturer in Art in Education, Goldsmiths College, University of London

John Jessel Lecturer in Education, Goldsmiths College, University of London

Susan Kendall Lecturer in Primary Education (RE), Goldsmiths College, University of London

Anna Mallett Postgraduate Student, Geography Department, Hertford College, Oxford University

Margaret Mallett Senior Lecturer at Goldsmiths College, University of London

Preface

This book is very much a group effort. It grew out of lively meetings between the contributors where we hammered out its shape and content. During that time we gradually emerged as editors.

One thing all contributors have in common is a commitment to the process of education and a direct experience of the pace of change. This now involves us in a continual restructuring of our courses and ideas. Initial and post-graduate teacher education students and those involved in continuing professional development or higher degree work are continually challenged to take more control of, and responsibility for, their learning. Contact time with tutors or supervisors reduces so new ways have to be found to continue to provide appropriate support. It is out of this challenge and responsibility that this book has grown. It is also a record of *our* learning and development as we try to lead, support and inspire in teacher education.

We hope this book will be useful and meet the needs we perceived during its conception and realisation.

Steve Herne
John Jessel
Jenny Griffiths

1 Study

Some guiding principles

John Jessel

Introduction

It may sound straightforward to say that the aim of studying is to learn. If learning consisted of one type of activity that was easy to define then a short prescription for effective study might be relatively easy to produce. However, if you pause for only a moment to consider the kinds of learning that you draw on during the course of a day then it is likely that you will think of quite a variety. Box 1.1 lists a few.

Box 1.1 Some examples of the kinds of learning used in the course of a day

- knowing how to perform various skills or carry out various procedures
- being able to solve problems
- knowing when to apply a theory or knowledge that you already have
- knowing which strategies to use or how to manage information
- having recall of items such as names, numbers, and a variety of other facts
- thinking critically
- being analytical
- communicating effectively
- being able to make informed decisions.

Diversity in learning has implications for the nature of study. As well as recalling information when needed, study is as much about developing the ability to use information effectively, to make decisions, to think imaginatively, creatively and critically, and to be sensitive to situations where these qualities are applicable. If your area of study is relevant to teaching and education then the range of what you need to learn can be extensive. You may not only have to embrace different subject disciplines that form part of the school curriculum but also to become familiar with a variety of educational issues and be prepared to draw on areas such as sociology and psychology that are relevant to learning and working with others in the classroom.

What is expected of study is subject to continual change. Ideas and understandings change, as do political and social demands. The nature of study can also be influenced by the availability of new technologies and the way these technologies are used. As part of, or as a result of, a course of study you may need to seek information from a variety of sources in a variety of forms. Likewise, you may need to communicate your ideas in ways which may vary from addressing an audience to creating text and moving images for use over a world-wide computer network. What is expected from study can also change as ideas about the nature of knowledge change. If the knowledge generated by a given community is regarded as unassailable, rather than tentative or subject to debate, then this in turn can have implications for how you approach your work. The circumstances under which people study and the stresses that these might impose can also be of concern. Issues such as these are addressed in later chapters. When you study, for whatever purpose, your efforts to learn are intentional and it is likely that you will want to do this effectively and feel that you have some control over the outcome. With this in mind, in the present chapter I aim to bring together some ideas about learning, to identify some principles arising from these and to outline what they mean in practice.

What do we know about learning?

Learning can be elusive; sometimes it just appears to happen while at other times, and in spite of much effort, it just seems to slip away. We know very little about how the brain works, and the mental processes that go on inside us cannot be directly observed. One response to this has been to avoid speculating about the unobservable and instead consider only behaviours which are observable. Behaviourists have taken this approach and regard learning in terms of repeated reinforcement of actions which can be associated with such stimuli as words, pictures and objects. If you were to follow a fully fledged behaviourist course of learning then your diet would consist of an area of pre-existing content or knowledge. This would be broken down into a series of smaller parts or competences presented in the form of a sequence or 'program', beginning with items deemed to be more basic and building up into more complex ones. Your learning could then be assessed in terms of observable outcomes or changes of behaviour, such as the ability to recall content or carry out a given procedure. Even if you did not follow a behaviourist program in its entirety, learning principles such as simple repetition, feedback and reinforcement through external reward would feature strongly. Learning in this case is assumed to be a matter of building on earlier behaviours: a quantitative increase in the knowledge and procedures at your disposal.

In contrast to focusing on our observable behaviours, learning can be viewed in terms of how we represent knowledge and develop our concepts and understandings. The term 'cognition' has been applied to this, and early cognitive approaches were based upon people reporting on their own mental experiences and activities. However, such 'introspective' methods have been widely criticised as subjective, being open to bias and disagreement which is difficult to resolve (e.g. Neisser 1976). Even though any underlying mental processes and structures are not directly observable, cognitive theories can have credibility if they are stated in such a way that they can be tested. Mayer (1981) draws the analogy that if a science based upon the strictly observable was applied to areas such as chemistry or physics then there would be no theory of atomic structure; although the parts which are thought to make up an atom cannot be seen, a theory of atoms has been used to make many useful predictions, many of which have practical significance.

Over the last few decades cognitive theories and the methods used to investigate them have proliferated, and figures such as Piaget and Vygotsky are well known for their work on how cognition develops within the individual, and the social effects upon this. Within this domain lies the notion of constructivism. Constructivist theory has been developed and interpreted in a number of ways and can provide a useful framework for understanding learning. In the sections which follow, some constructivist approaches are introduced and applied to the process of studying.

Constructivism and learning

According to constructivist theory, we form mental representations or 'constructions' as a result of our experience of the world around us. There may be representations of objects such as a table or an ice cream, or events such as breakfast or journeying home. Some representations may appear more abstract, such as profit or fitness, and there is scope for representations to become relatively complex. Such representations form the basis of our knowledge or understandings. At first our understandings may be limited; a table may be regarded as a particular object at home, rather than just one example of a variety of similar objects that we may encounter later on and from which the more general concept of a table may be built. Our ideas and understandings can interrelate so that we build up both a more complex and a more coherent mental picture, or body of knowledge. Constructivist theory regards learning in terms of the continual building and development of mental structures. Sometimes progress may be smooth, in the sense that we continue to elaborate upon an existing idea or structure by incorporating information that is largely consistent with it – assimilation, in Piagetian terms. On other occasions the journey is less smooth and new experiences do not fit neatly into any existing structures. One effect of this can be that we choose to ignore such experiences for a while, or even bend our perception of them in order to fit our existing understandings, until we reach a point when a new structure has to be created in order to make sense of things in a different way – the Piagetian notion of accommodation. To take a familiar example: once upon a time it was thought that the sun, the moon and the stars revolved around the earth – that is how people saw it and explained it. In time, new observations did not fit easily with this explanation and a different representation or understanding of a solar system had to be formed; the position of the earth was seen differently. An important point that emerges from this is that learning is not just a matter of adding to our knowledge – there will be times in the course of our studies when we will have to abandon existing ideas and find other ways of seeing or thinking about things. Learning is to do with qualitative rather than merely quantitative change.

Key points

- Constructivists see learning in terms of creating and developing mental structures.
- Learning is about understanding things differently – not just remembering more information.

Mental structures can help us make sense of the mass of surrounding information. Understanding can be helped if relevant structures are 'activated' by prior knowledge. This has been illustrated by a series of experiments carried out by Bransford and Johnson (1972, 1973). In one experiment passages of text similar to that in Box 1.2 were read to three groups of college students. (Before going any further you may wish to read the passage and rate your comprehension of it.)

Box 1.2 An example of a passage of text used by Bransford and Johnson (1972: 722) for investigating the effect of prior knowledge on understanding and recall

The procedure is actually quite simple. First you arrange items into different groups. Of course one pile may be sufficient depending on how

> much there is to do. If you have to go somewhere else due to lack of facilities that is the next step; otherwise, you are pretty well set. It is important not to overdo things. That is, it is better to do too few things at once than too many. In the short run this may not seem important but complications can easily arise. A mistake can be expensive as well. At first, the whole procedure will seem complicated. Soon, however, it will become just another facet of life. It is difficult to foresee any end to the necessity for this task in the immediate future, but then, one never can tell. After the procedure is completed one arranges the materials into different groups again. Then they can be put into their appropriate places. Eventually they will be used once more and the whole cycle will then have to be repeated. However, that is part of life.

One group was given no other information, the second was told beforehand what the text was about (washing clothes, in the above example) and a third group was told the topic afterwards. In comparison to the students in the other groups, those who were given the topic in advance not only found the text easier to understand but also recalled more of the content when tested. It should also be noted that a topic such as washing clothes would not have been unfamiliar to the students who took part; the point here is that activation of already established mental structures was helpful. Bransford and Johnson (1972) obtained similar results with regard to comprehension when a picture was used to provide a context for interpreting text. In some ways this is comparable to one of those occasions when you unpack something, such as a chair, which arrives in many pieces which you have to assemble. Following the sequence of accompanying written instructions can be helped if you look on the packaging for a picture of the assembled item.

Although the above experiments were highly contrived, some study strategies are nevertheless suggested. For example, the overall framework provided by a topic heading, a diagram or the title of a lecture should be given some thought beforehand, or, if you know this well in advance, it may also help comprehension and memory if you try to recall and note down what you already know about the topic. Similarly, it is helpful to scan text or other forms of learning material in advance, taking note of such basic features as headings, and looking for any familiar concepts in order to get a general idea of the topic.

The idea of using an overall framework in learning has been developed by Svensson (1977, 1984). He places emphasis on the learning of organised wholes, contrasting what is termed a 'holistic' approach in studying with an 'atomistic' approach. How you organise parts into a whole is important; it is not any kind of grouping or ordering. The organising principle used is likely to depend on what is to be learned, but could include identifying such things as the main parts of an argument, supporting evidence and conclusion, a main principle and example, a narrative, and cause and effect. For example, once you have a sense of where the argument is going, then it is easier to understand the details on the way. While isolated details and facts can be of little consequence, they can take on importance if related meaningfully to an overall structure. Holistic approaches become important with more complex learning, particularly with regard to understanding and, incidentally, maintaining interest.

The idea of gaining an overall picture while studying will recur in other ways in this chapter. Although topic headings and overall organising structures can be helpful, there is also a cautionary note in that if you aim to learn from what you read or listen to, then, rather than being under the illusion that you have an entire knowledge of the content, it is important to be on the lookout for information which departs from your expectations.

Key points

Understanding and remembering what you listen to or read can be helped if you:

- take careful note of titles and topic headings *beforehand*;
- brainstorm the topic *beforehand*;
- keep sight of the overall picture.

Making connections

If our minds consisted of a mass of unconnected or isolated concepts then constructing meanings would be difficult. Building and developing mental structures is about making connections. The connections we make are seldom random or haphazard; as learners we link ideas and information so that what is new is integrated with what is already familiar. To a large extent we do this naturally as we experience the world about us. However, if numerous academic demands are made while studying, effective integration can become more difficult as one has less time to make links with existing knowledge, so that new concepts or information can become isolated. In practice this means that it is important to find time (and it does take time) to recall earlier ideas and link these, for example by making comparisons and contrasts.

Finding new relationships and making multiple connections between ideas also have implications for enriching our understanding and seeing things differently. Again, to take a familiar example, at a relatively basic level our understanding of ‘hot’ becomes more developed if it is related not only to a variety of things which produce heat but also to the effects of heat, and to our experience of 'cold'. At a more abstract level we may seek to understand the distinction between heat and temperature but still make connections to concrete examples, such as whether or not a spark from a fire, which is at a relatively high temperature, contains more heat than the cup of tea which has just been poured out. Making a variety of connections, including those between different levels of abstraction, helps understanding. One consequence of this for study has been identified by White (1988), who advocates that it is better to seek multiple and varied situations that permit exploration and re-exploration of a concept, revisiting it regularly, than to try to seek a once-and-for-all-time definitive or perfect explanation or activity.

Mental structure is also important for memory. Having a good memory does not only rely on how permanently you store information, it also depends on how easily you can gain access to that information when you want it. As our mental structures become established they can allow efficient storage and access to information. Having more interconnections between ideas also means more possible routes to particular memories. Another way of looking at this is that remembering is not always helped by paring things down to a bare minimum.

Key points

Understanding and remembering can be helped if you:

- take time to make links between ideas;
- take time to compare and contrast ideas;
- take time to make links between theory and practical examples.

Models, metaphors and analogies

Using models is an example of making connections in our thinking. Something that we are already familiar with can help us construct an understanding of something else. We can apply our knowledge of one field to help solve a problem in another field. Models can take a variety of forms; they can be diagrammatic, mathematical and verbal as well as physical. Analogies and metaphors are everyday examples of models used to draw connections between concepts. Books such as Black's (1962) *Models as Metaphors* and Jones's (1982) *Physics as Metaphor* are examples of an extensive and established literature which acknowledges the importance of metaphors as part of our thinking. In some cases a close similarity, as in 'sand runs through your fingers like water', can be helpful when representing an idea. In other cases a novel or more creative step may be taken, as in 'language is a window on our thoughts', or even 'study is a game'. Although the connected items have some features in common, a measure of dissimilarity frequently encountered with the metaphor is important in the construction of new meanings. Having established a connection, in order to develop your ideas it is important to refine the structure that has been created by looking for differences or distinguishing features. Although 'the brain as computer' may act as a starting point which can provide some useful insights, it can, if taken too far and too literally, give rise to some severely limiting and simplistic notions. An important point to remember is that models are not 'reality': they are created for a purpose, at best are likely to contain only a few features relating to that purpose, and in the end will have limitations. What appears initially to be a useful model can turn out to be a misleading one, and you may therefore need to be prepared to be flexible and seek out and try alternatives. In short, models, analogies and metaphors can help focus attention so that we can develop understandings and solve problems but, as with many other tools, they should be chosen and handled with care!

Key points

- If you use a model or an analogy then what you know in one area can help you with another area.
- A model is created for a particular purpose and is unlikely to represent every aspect of a situation.

Being an active learner

An enduring theme in constructivist approaches is the importance of active involvement in the creation and development of mental structures. Being active means being mentally active – for example, looking for patterns and making predictions, testing ideas and solving problems. Mental activity also involves an interaction with our existing knowledge structures; we extend, refine and reformulate earlier ideas. Physical activity, of course, may be involved in working through ideas if we handle and observe objects or use models – but co-existent with this is mental activity. Through becoming mentally active you can take control of your own learning. By way of contrast, you would be taking a passive approach if you fed yourself with information, such as through reading every word of a book or article uncritically, seeing the contents in isolation and not making connections with your own thinking. Being passive also means trying to memorise information rather than trying to derive something from it that can be used. Being passive means not using your own mind.

The term 'generative study strategies' has been applied to the process of developing mental structures through active involvement so that information undergoes transformation (Peper and Meyer 1986; Lahtinen *et al.* 1997). Through taking an active approach, you can use existing knowledge and abilities to transform information and ideas and produce or 'generate' such things as summaries, graphs and diagrams to represent concepts, essays, role plays, internal or imaginary models and concept maps, and to investigate and create solutions to problems (Kafai and Resnick 1996). The potential of using generative study strategies in conjunction with information technology is discussed in Chapter 7.

Reading can be made active through having a clear sense of purpose, identifying questions concerning what you need to know so that particular targets can be searched for. Active reading has been developed by Davies and Greene (1984). Although they aimed their work at pupils in secondary schools, the principles apply to any level of study. They regard it as important to put forward your own ideas before checking them against the text, being ready to modify your initial interpretations, and, finally, not forgetting to refer to any diagrams or other visual material in parallel with reference to the text. By way of contrast, non-generative or 'reproductive' strategies, where text is simply copied through activities such as passive reading, are likely to be less effective in conceptual development. Underlining or copying sections of text are typical examples of 'reproductive' strategies because no reorganisation of ideas is necessary. Similarly, setting yourself a target such as to read and make notes from the next ten pages before lunchtime is too general and is unlikely to stimulate active mental processing.

One generative study strategy based upon making connections is to create a concept map. An example is shown in Figure 1.3, and a further one is given in Chapter 4. One or two words can be used as a term to represent each idea or concept. Typically there might be at least half a dozen such terms. The idea is to place those terms that are more closely related nearer to each other. Lines are then drawn between those terms where a relationship is seen, and the nature of the relationship summarised alongside. Some maps may turn out to be web-like in structure, others tree-like; and if you are trying to sequence ideas to develop an argument, a more linear structure or flow may prevail. Concept maps be used in the process of brainstorming and to help organise and develop ideas (e.g. Novak and Godwin 1984; White and Gunstone 1992), and to help critically review printed articles (Lonka *et al.* 1994). Concept mapping can also lead to effective recall as well as understanding (Novak 1990; Okebukola 1992; Catchpole and Garland 1996). Mapping your ideas can allow you to gain an overview of an area and is an example of the holistic approach mentioned earlier.

Concept mapping can be used as a diagrammatic form of note-taking. Although this may be relatively easily achieved with a book or an article, the conditions for taking notes are very different during a lecture or watching a video. In the latter circumstances making notes has to be done while listening and deciding what to note – all within a limited period of time. For this reason note-taking during lectures may not always be effective in allowing one to transform and process

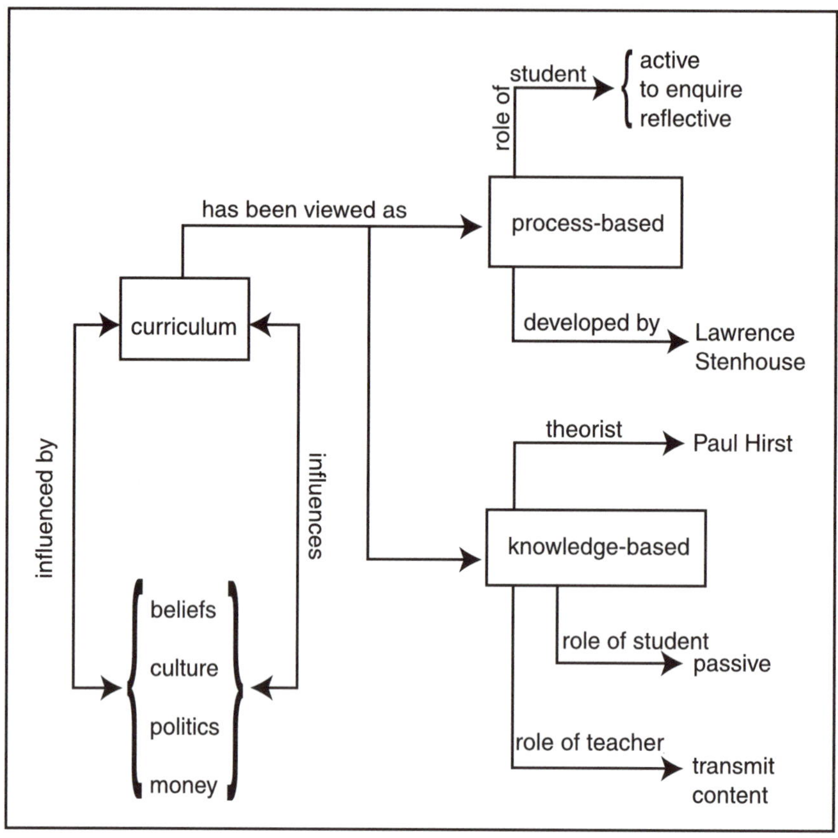

Figure 1.1 An example of a concept map

ideas effectively. Although studies such as those by Kiewra *et al.* (1989, 1991) have found that when such generative strategies are used during lectures recall is better, this may not always be the case. For example, specific wording may be crucial with some subject matter, and there have been occasions when college students have felt that unless they were noting verbatim there was the potential for the original meaning to become distorted and their notes confused (Van Meter *et al.* 1994). There is, of course, a certain security in taking notes, in that one has a record to refer to, and many people automatically do it. Indeed, it has been found that any type of note-taking is an aid to producing a more coherent account in comparison to not making notes at all (Lahtinen *et al.* 1997; Peper and Meyer 1986).

Key points

Understanding and remembering can be helped if you make learning active by:

- looking for patterns, making predictions, testing ideas and solving problems;
- translating ideas into different forms, e.g. words, diagrams, pictures, graphs;
- giving reading a purpose by identifying what you are looking for in advance.

Deep and surface approaches to learning

There is evidence to suggest that how much we remember varies according to the type of task which is set. In a classic series of experiments Craik and Tulving (1975) asked people questions about lists of words: for example, whether a particular word was in capital letters (e.g. STREET/street), whether or not each word belonged to a particular category of meaning (e.g. food, animal), or whether each word would fit into a given sentence (e.g. 'He sat down to eat at the ...'). Afterwards a surprise test was given to see how many of the original words were recognised when mixed up with other words. It was found that people could more accurately indicate the words that they had seen before if those words had been categorised in terms of their meaning or included as part of a sentence, rather than being categorised in terms of capital letters (which convey information in terms of visual shape rather than meaning). Although interpreting the results of their experiments is problematic, Craik and Tulving's work has given rise to many other studies investigating the idea that finding meaning improves both recognition and recall. For example, pictures are more likely to be recognised if one is asked to interpret what they mean (Meudell *et al.* 1980), as are pictures of faces if judged in such terms as honesty and friendliness rather than more specific features such as nose size (Bower and Karlin 1974).

The ways in which university students approach learning in terms of depth of meaning and the types of learning outcome obtained have been extensively investigated by Marton and Säljö (1976, 1984). They found that students differed in terms of *what* they learned from a text rather than simply in terms of *how much* they learned. For example, while some students gained a sense of the author's intended argument, others, although recalling some details of the passage, gave accounts which suggested overall misconceptions. In other words, the text was understood in qualitatively different ways, the former being described as more deep and the latter as less deep. Correspondingly, with regard to the learning approaches used by the students, two clearly distinguishable levels of processing were identified: a deep level and a surface level. Surface-level processing was characterised by a preoccupation with remembering as much of the text as possible, such as facts, figures, names and examples. With deep-level processing the emphasis was on focusing on the point of the text: the author's intention, the main message and the conclusion to be drawn. In effect the students were trying to do different things, and it was found, perhaps unsurprisingly, that deep-level processing related to deeper levels of learning outcome and vice versa. Although the emphasis may appear to be on meaning and understanding, Ramsden (1992) notes that the issue is not about learning facts versus learning concepts; rather, it is about attempting to learn unrelated facts and procedures as opposed to learning facts or procedures *in relation to* concepts. Putting factual information into a meaningful framework helps you to recall that information.

In practice, we may adopt both deep and surface approaches according to our perception of the nature of the task in hand, how we think we are going to be assessed, our familiarity with the area, and as a result of the learning context (Laurillard 1984). Surface approaches can arise from over-anxiety to perform well, and also appear to be linked to extrinsic motives, such as in trying to meet the demands made by others (Fransson 1977). Many of the attributes of a deep approach can appear to happen naturally – for example, in everyday situations where a topic is seen to have personal interest or relevance. In other words, this can be associated with intrinsic motives. The point here is that we all have the capability of adopting a deep approach; it is up to us to exploit this effectively.

Some characteristics of deep- and surface-level processing drawn from work reported by Marton and Säljö (1976, 1984) are summarised in Box 1.4. Although some of the statements partly overlap, I have nevertheless included them because the different wordings may be helpful if you try to link these with your own study techniques. With regard to the deep-level approaches, phrases such as 'stop and think' and 'stop and consider' emphasise that it can take time to reflect; reading is not a race. While the list may appear to be helpful, there is also a precautionary message which arises from Marton and Säljö's (1984) work with regard to adopting a deep approach as part of one's study strategies. They tried to encourage a deep approach in reading by, for example, asking students to summarise sub-sections in an introductory chapter of a book and to state the relationship between each sub-section. They found that the students read the text so that they were able to mention the contents superficially, rather than with the critical reflectivity characteristic of a deep approach. In other words, it is possible to summarise but to do so without understanding: the summary became an end in itself. This may have been due to the predictability of the demands of the learning situation or how the demands were interpreted, rather than intended. Another influencing factor suggested was an ingrained cultural attitude about learning from texts which is reproductive in nature; students' conceptions of learning ranged from the acquisition of knowledge regarded as fact to be retained to learning as an interpretative process. In the final chapter I will discuss the importance of students and teachers sharing and communicating their conceptions of learning, rather than simply assuming these. In sum, adopting a deep approach may require time and effort, and the techniques in tutorial texts or materials in such formats as the CD-ROM may need to be regarded critically if superficiality is to be avoided.

Box 1.3 Characteristics of deep- and surface-level processing

When using deep-level approaches, students:

- look for the main message and try to understand the point of it;
- stop and think about what the author wants to say;
- try to look for the principal ideas;
- consider what they think about the ideas and arguments;
- consider how the ideas and arguments have been built up;
- stop and consider if there is something they think is not right;
- stop and consider if one part logically follows another part;
- look for links between the text and other things they have read or experienced;
- consider their own feelings about the issues raised;
- recognise that as a result of reading they might think along different lines;
- are driven by their own wish to make sense of the world.

When using surface-level approaches, students:

- concentrate on trying to remember as much as possible;
- try to get in as much reading as possible;
- feel under pressure of time;
- try to remember isolated facts, figures and names;
- become distracted by thinking about how much they have to remember;
- try to concentrate so hard that they find it difficult to think and interpret;
- are driven by the thought of being tested or extrinsically rewarded rather than through interest in the topic.

(Summarised and adapted from Marton and Säljö 1976, 1984)

Using language

Language can be used to represent our experiences and ideas, and as a means of communication. Although constructivists have put different emphases on the way that they interpret these roles, each interpretation nevertheless draws attention to another way that language can help us in the course of study. For Piaget (1980) mental structures are gained through first-hand interaction or manipulation of objects, and verbal, or symbolic, representation occurs subsequent to this intellectual development. For Vygotsky (1962), language plays a central role in thinking. Initially, thoughts may occur without the involvement of words and, conversely, words may be used without being understood. However, at an early stage both become dependent on each other and support each other's development. An 'inner dialogue' is regarded as important in transforming the way we understand. When our ideas are represented 'symbolically' through language they can be manipulated without having to rely on direct experience with things. This more 'formal' way of thinking allows us to use ideas for new purposes, to combine or put our thoughts together in logical patterns, to reason or develop arguments, to make deductions, predictions and hypotheses, and, in turn, to construct further meanings. In practice, the words and forms of linguistic expression that we choose reflect a central part of our thinking and have implications for how we develop our ideas. Using language carefully and considering the language that others use critically, then, is part of the process of study.

There are differing views on the part that language can play in the development of understandings through communication. For example, conflict can arise within discussion; you may discover that your ideas are at variance with those of others. A contradiction, however, is something that can be usefully explored. Rather than this being seen as a matter of who is right and who is wrong, it can be helpful to reflect on how a particular viewpoint was arrived at and the assumptions or conceptions that gave rise to it (Fosnot 1996). More generally within a social setting there are those such as Schifter and Simon (1992) who argue that the 'dissonances' encountered in the course of negotiating a shared meaning can allow individuals to develop by restructuring their concepts. With regard to your own study, this suggests that you should make use of any formal or informal opportunities for discussion. How you work within these settings is important. Exploring contradicting ideas requires co-operation from all parties; for example, this means listening to and respecting each other's viewpoints. In their work on a constructivist approach to discussions, Carter *et al.* (1997) point out the value of raising questions and risk-taking in putting forward ideas.

In contrast to allowing learning to arise from conflict, language can also promote learning through communicating generally accepted understandings by a given community. These can be passed on by those deemed more knowledgeable, so that learners can move on more quickly than if left to their own devices. The relevance of formalised knowledge within the adult academic context is argued forcefully by Laurillard (1993), who regards the focus of academic learning to be not the world itself but others' view of that world. She states that 'knowledge has to be abstracted, and represented formally, in order to become generalisable and therefore more generally useful' (ibid.: 20). Vygotsky (1978) regards learning through instruction as fundamental to development. However, this does not imply a simple 'transmission' model of learning, since account is taken of the concepts that are constructed 'spontaneously' from one's own everyday experience and how they may relate to those that are formalised and more widely accepted within a given culture. When considering children's learning, Vygotsky (1962) argued that if spontaneous concepts have reached a certain level so that they fall within what is termed a 'zone of proximal development' then, with support from a more knowledgeable adult or peer, such concepts can be linked to more formal versions and deployed more effectively. Applied more generally in terms of study strategies, this suggests that learning from an authoritative source is more likely to be effective if you already have some related experience which you have reflected upon, and have begun to construct your own ideas. It emphasises the importance of engaging in a variety of relevant activities, such as testing out ideas in practice, solving problems, choosing the appropriate level of reading material, and generally familiarising yourself with a topic in preparation for a lecture.

Language takes on a further dimension if it is recorded. For example, if we are able to represent our thoughts in writing then they can be re-examined and reflected upon. Although an obvious function of writing is to remind us of our ideas at a later date, a more important function with regard to our developing ideas is that writing helps unburden the memory; words can act as mental cues, marking out our thoughts so that we can reconsider and build upon them, or attend to further lines of thinking. If you wish to take advantage of writing in this way then what you write initially is unlikely to be a final product. In effect, you will make a rough draft, work with that draft and be prepared to make changes to it as your thoughts progress. Howard (1990) contrasts the distinction between this 'process-oriented' view of writing and a 'product-oriented' view, where the intention is solely to communicate. He argues that the primary goal of writing is to understand, and only then to make that understanding available to others. In practice, the two different functions of writing can be obscured by too readily regarding writing as communication: preoccupation with the final result can be inhibiting in that it can be assumed that everything has got to be right first time.

Although verbal language may appear to dominate when studying, it is only one example of an intellectual tool. Other forms of representation, such as diagrams and physical or mathematical models, can be instrumental in the process of thinking. Each medium we use has its own attributes and limitations and, as Fosnot (1996) suggests, this in turn is likely to have an effect both on what ideas, things or events around us are represented and on how they are represented. For example, she cites Sherman's (1978) observations that children are likely to represent buildings when using plastic foam, and people and animals when using clay. Olson's (1970) demonstration is also cited: namely, when using words people tend to describe a cup in terms of its function, with pencil and paper the handle and side, and with clay the inside and outside contours. To a scientist such as Leonardo da Vinci, drawing was an important tool in the process of understanding all manner of things in the surrounding world. With regard to your own study, using different forms of representation can enable new connections between ideas to be made, and in turn this has implications for conceptual development and memory. Information technology provides further possibilities with regard to representation, and these are discussed in Chapter 7.

Key points

- Use language carefully – it is an important part of your thinking, not an extra.
- Discussion helps you to learn through exploring different or contradicting viewpoints.
- Learning from being told is helped if you have already developed some of your own ideas.
- Writing can be used to mark out your thoughts and ideas so that you can build upon them.
- Be prepared to make changes in your writing as your understanding develops.
- Using diagrams, models and other forms of representation can help you develop ideas.

Thinking critically

Academic life is composed of many imperfect ingredients. Making progress in our thinking and understanding of the world may not always result from applying well-established computational rules. Much of what we think we know is tentative or subject to uncertainty. For example, words such as 'prove' or 'disprove' are generally not regarded as acceptable parts of scientific currency – at best we may find evidence that supports, or does not support, a given argument or theory. Familiar concepts such as intelligence and personality are deeply contested, and can be seen to be little more than convenience terms to represent people's ideas. Although there are many theories about intelligence, we cannot say for sure that such an entity exists. The extensive philosophical debates about the nature of knowledge are well known. For example, Popper (1969) regards progress in science to be made through falsification of theory, and Kuhn (1970) sees progress in terms of shifts in our understandings in response to a build-up of observations and experimental results which do not fit existing theories, so that new ways of looking at the world are put forward. Thomas (1997) points out that, in education, theory is often regarded as creed-like and not as a tenuous or loose statement that is open to refutation. He also argues that ideas on what is theory in education are in themselves confused.

Study in education is inevitably carried out in relation to a backdrop of different ideas, many of them competing, complex and untidy. Inconsistencies in argument, lack of evidence, fallacy and distortion are part of academic life. Trying to be aware of these is an important part of taking a critical approach to your work. Ryan (1984) has found that students who regard knowledge as a framework for interpreting information are more likely to attain higher course grades than students who regard knowledge in terms of a set of absolute truths or facts which they must seek out and learn. An important part of critical thinking is exploring different interpretations of ideas and observations. This means treating ideas tentatively rather than seeking a hard and fast 'absolute' rule (Langer and Piper 1987). It can help, for example, to ask yourself what something *could be* or *could mean* rather than simply what something *is* or *means*.

Critical thinking is regarded by Halpern (1998) as involving higher-order cognitive skills. Such skills cannot simply be applied by rote. It is necessary to take the context and a range of other factors into account. This is a reflective process and requires judgement, analysis and synthesis (ibid.: 451). She argues that critical thinking involves the deliberate use of skills and strategies which can be learned and transferred to new contexts. Similarly, Zechmeister and Johnson (1992) adopt an approach where guiding principles can be identified. McPeck (1981) takes an alternative stance on some of these issues, arguing, for example, that general critical thinking skills are difficult to formulate, and that transfer from one domain of knowledge to another cannot be assumed. He sees critical thinking in terms of engaging in an activity with 'reflective scepticism': one has to know when to raise a question and what questions to ask, and this requires knowledge of a field and the beliefs which form its underlying foundations.

One notable attempt to specify critical thinking skills has been made by Ennis (1962). His list includes making judgements on whether there is ambiguity in reasoning, whether statements contradict each other, whether a conclusion follows necessarily, whether something is an assumption and whether a definition is adequate. Among the critical thinking skills which Halpern (1998: 452) regards as teachable and generalisable are 'understanding how cause is determined, recognizing and criticizing assumptions' and 'giving reasons to support a conclusion, assessing degrees of likelihood and uncertainty, incorporating isolated data into a wider framework, and using analogies to solve problems'. She also recognises a creative component in that alternatives may have to be generated and selected, with judgements made among them. Verbal reasoning can play a large part in this, with arguments having to be comprehended and analysed.

McPeck's (1981) argument that any ability to be critical in one area may not automatically apply to another is echoed in Halpern's (1998) observation that the ability to recognise when to apply a skill in novel situations is critical and can be an Achilles' heel. However, Halpern suggests that problems of transfer can arise because there are no obvious cues in a new context that can trigger relevant critical thinking skills. In view of this, she places emphasis on identifying the underlying structure of a problem or argument (rather than the topic it relates to) so that this can be used as a means of jogging the memory. Here the constructivist principle of developing connections between knowledge structures is applicable, in that recall is more likely to occur when a given concept is given a deeper meaning by being linked to other concepts. To this end, Halpern suggests such tasks as drawing a diagram or other form of graphical notation to organise information, and finding more than one way of stating or solving a problem.

Brookfield (1995) has considered the nature of assumptions in some detail. He describes these as beliefs about the world that seem so obvious that they do not need to be stated explicitly. Because of this, becoming aware of our assumptions is difficult. Three broad categories of assumptions have been identified: paradigmatic, prescriptive and causal. Causal assumptions are often stated in terms of a prediction: for example, 'lecturing induces passivity and kills critical thinking'. These are often the easiest to detect. Prescriptive assumptions are concerned with what we think should be happening in a particular situation: for example, 'if adults are believed to be self-directed learners then the best teaching will encourage their taking control over designing, conducting and evaluating their own learning'. Paradigmatic assumptions are about the fundamental categories we use to make sense of our world: for example, 'progressive teaching methods are more democratic than traditional ones'. Brookfield (1995) regards paradigmatic assumptions as the most difficult to detect, and challenging them can often be met with resistance. In his book he develops the idea of 'hunting assumptions'. This can be approached through considering examples of 'common sense' assumptions and their implications, along with alternative interpretations which challenge the validity of the initial assumptions. It is the continual attempt to see things differently that is regarded as central to reflection. Critical reflection for Brookfield also involves a political dimension: for example, through recognising dominant cultural values. Mezirow (1991) considers critical reflection in a less overtly political manner in terms of a 'perspective transformation' resulting from a recognition and critique of the perspectives, beliefs and attitudes formed in relation to the mental structures that we develop. His theory of transformative learning takes account of the way the structures we create influence how we interpret experience, the dynamics involved when we modify meanings, and the way structures themselves undergo change when we find that they no longer work for us.

It is also widely recognised that critical thinking involves not only logical and intellectual abilities but also attitude or disposition. Halpern (1998), for example, notes that critical thinking requires effort and willingness, rather than just ability. Similarly, D'Angelo (1971) has identified such characteristics as intellectual curiosity, open-mindedness, persistence and a respect for other viewpoints. Being critical can also involve reflecting upon and assessing our own thinking; a 'metacognitive' component which is now discussed.

Key points

- Knowledge can be regarded as open to interpretation rather than as a truth which must be learned.
- Critical thinking can involve such skills as recognising assumptions, ambiguity and contradiction.
- Critical thinking not only involves logical and intellectual abilities but also involves such qualities as curiosity, open-mindedness, persistence, respect for other viewpoints and willingness to put in effort.

Metacognition

Metacognition is about being aware of, reflecting on and managing our thinking. Metacognition is relevant to studying and learning in that it is concerned with making explicit our understandings of how we acquire our knowledge and understandings, and using that information to guide us in improving our learning. In many ways this chapter is about just that. However, the topic of metacognition warrants particular mention because it places emphasis on the benefits of continuing to be mindful in actively managing and developing study activities rather than merely carrying them out automatically. Effective metacognitive activity can be thought of as a kind of 'self-interrogation' and 'self-regulation' (Brown and DeLoache 1983). These are conscious acts which involve such basic skills as predicting the consequences of an action or event, checking the results and examining one's own activity in the process of this. For example, when considering the design of science courses for teacher education, Mayer-Smith and Mitchell suggest that metacognition can be approached by:

> monitoring one's personal understanding (e.g. 'Is this sentence meaningful to me?'),
> monitoring one's current conceptions (e.g. 'What view of forces am I using here?'),
> monitoring the meaning of a communication (e.g. 'What was the main idea in this paragraph?'),

> monitoring one's progress against instructions (e.g. 'Have I done everything specified?'), and
> monitoring one's progress against intentions (e.g. 'Why did I begin this problem by calculating the [amount] of HCl remaining in the flask?').
>
> (Mayer-Smith and Mitchell 1997: 133)

The above examples of monitoring are, of course, widely applicable to learning in any field. At a more general management level, metacognition can mean being clear about the nature of the learning task, asking yourself whether you are staying on task, and considering how you will know when you have achieved your aims. If you do think that you have achieved your aims then you may need to check this. For example, you may need to try to explain or recall something without any form of prompting, or find some way of testing to find out what you do know and what you don't know. This is particularly pertinent in view of Glenberg *et al.*'s (1982) findings that students are susceptible to an 'illusion of knowing'; believing they have understood something when this has not been the case. We can be prone to what they call the 'default assumption', where we assume that we understand something unless we get signals to the contrary. When reading, for example, it is a question of finding a balance between making predictions from our overall idea of what the text is about and not jumping to premature conclusions on what might have been said. It means making active and meaningful elaborations and distinctions between the ideas that are presented; if you need to re-read a passage of text you should not be deterred from this because of feelings about being inefficient as a reader. Being aware that understanding is something that has to be worked towards and that re-reading and pondering statements is part of reading actively are examples of part of the metacognitive process. It can also help to talk about your thinking, or even keep a diary of the process. These activities help you to develop a vocabulary, and to identify and be articulate about the skills or strategies that you use, so that you can evaluate yourself as a learner.

Postscript

In this chapter I have outlined a view of learning based on the development and refinement of mental structures and used this to provide a basis for developing study strategies. Although constructivist principles are often encountered in relation to children's learning and the role of the teacher, the emphasis has been on the idea that what is encountered in the classroom can equally apply to your own learning. Although constructivism can provide an overall conceptual framework, it is only a theory. As such it is inevitably subject to interpretation, debate and ongoing development; it cannot provide a series of certainties or a quick fix.

Nevertheless, I hope what has been outlined will act as a prelude to interpreting the chapters which follow.

References

Benton, S.L., Kiewra, K.A., Whitfill, J.M. and Dennison, R. (1993) 'Encoding and external-storage effects on writing processes', *Journal of Educational Psychology* 85: 267–80.

Black, M. (1962) *Models as Metaphors*, New York: Cornell University Press.

Bower, G.H. and Karlin, M.B. (1974) 'Depth processing pictures of faces and recognition memory', *Journal of Experimental Psychology* 103: 751–7.

Bransford, J.D. and Johnson, M.K. (1972) 'Contextual prerequisites for understanding: Some investigations of comprehension and recall', *Journal of Verbal Learning and Verbal Behaviour* 11: 717–26.

Bransford, J.D. and Johnson, M.K. (1973) 'Considerations of some problems of comprehension', in W.G. Chase (ed.) *Visual Information Processing*, New York: Academic Press.

Brookfield, S.D. (1995) *Becoming a Critically Reflective Teacher*, San Francisco CA: Jossey-Bass.

Brown, A.L. and DeLoache, J.S. (1983) 'Skills, plans and self-regulation', in M. Donaldson, R. Grieve and C. Pratt (eds) *Early Childhood Development and Education: Readings in Psychology*, Oxford: Blackwell.

Bruner, J.S. (1966) *Toward a Theory of Instruction*, Cambridge: Harvard University Press.

Carter, M., Ensrud, M. and Holden, J. (1997) 'The Paideia Seminar: a constructivist approach to discussions', *Teaching and Change* 5, 1: 32–49.

Catchpole, R. and Garland, N. (1996) 'Mind maps: using research to improve the student learning experience', in G. Gibbs (ed.) *Improving Student Learning – Using Research to Improve Student Learning*, Oxford: The Oxford Centre for Staff Development.

Craik, F.I.M. and Tulving, E. (1975) 'Depth of processing and the retention of words in episodic memory', *Journal of Experimental Psychology* General 104: 268–94.

D'Angelo, E. (1971) *The Teaching of Critical Thinking*, Amsterdam: B.R. Gruner.

Davies, F. and Greene, T. (1984) *Reading for Learning in the Sciences*, Edinburgh: Oliver and Boyd.

Ennis, R. (1962) 'A concept of critical thinking', *Harvard Educational Review* 32, 1: 83–111.

Fosnot, C.T. (1996) 'Constructivism: a psychological theory of learning', in C.T. Fosnot (ed.), *Constructivism: Theory, Perspectives, and Practice*, New York: Teachers College Press.

Fransson, A. (1977) 'On qualitative differences in learning. IX – Effects of motivation and test anxiety on process and outcome', *British Journal of Educational Psychology* 47: 244–57.

Glenberg, A.M., Wilkinson, A.C. and Epstein, W. (1982) 'The illusion of knowing: failure in the self-assessment of comprehension', *Memory and Cognition* 10: 597–602.

Halpern, D.F. (1998) 'Teaching critical thinking for transfer across domains', *American Psychologist* 53, 4: 449–55.

Howard, V.A. (1990) 'Thinking on paper: a philosopher's look at writing', in V.A. Howard (ed.) *Varieties of Thinking*, London: Routledge.

Jones, R. (1982) *Physics as Metaphor*, Minneapolis: University of Minnesota Press.

Kafai, Y. and Resnick, M. (1996) 'Introduction', in Y. Kafai and M. Resnick (eds) *Constructionism in Practice: Designing, Thinking, and Learning in a Digital World*, Hillsdale: Lawrence Erlbaum Associates.

Kiewra, K.A., DuBois, N.F., Christensen, M., Kim, S. and Lindberg, N. (1989) 'A more equitable account of the note-taking functions in learning from lecture and from text', *Journal of Instructional Science* 18: 217–32.

Kiewra, K.A., DuBois, N.F., Christian, D., McShane, A., Meyerhoffer, M. and Roskelley, D. (1991) 'Note-taking functions and techniques', *Journal of Educational Psychology* 83: 240–5.

Kuhn, T. (1970) *The Structure of Scientific Revolutions*, Chicago: University of Chicago Press.

Lahtinen, V., Lonka, K. and Lindblom-Ylänne, S. (1997) 'Spontaneous study strategies and the quality of knowledge construction', *British Journal of Educational Psychology* 67: 13–24.

Langer, E.J. and Piper, A.I. (1987) 'The prevention of mindlessness', *Journal of Personality and Social Psychology* 53: 280–7.

Laurillard, D. (1984) 'Learning from problem-solving', in F. Marton, D. Hounsell and N. Entwistle (eds) *The Experience of Learning*, Edinburgh: Scottish Academic Press.

Laurillard, D. (1993) *Rethinking University Teaching*, London: Routledge.

Lonka, K., Lindblom-Ylänne, S. and Maury, S. (1994) 'The effect of study strategies on learning from text', *Learning and Instruction* 4: 253–71.

McPeck, J.E. (1981) *Critical Thinking and Education*, Oxford: Martin Robertson.

Marton, F. and Säljö, R. (1976) 'On qualitative differences in learning: I. Outcome and process', *British Journal of Educational Psychology* 46: 4–11.

Marton, F. and Säljö, R. (1984) 'Approaches to learning', in F. Marton, D. Hounsell and N. Entwistle (eds) *The Experience of Learning*, Edinburgh: Scottish Academic Press.

Mayer, R.E. (1981) *The Promise of Cognitive Psychology*, San Francisco: W.H. Freeman and Company.

Mayer-Smith, J.A. and Mitchell, I.J. (1997) 'Teaching about constructivism: using approaches informed by constructivism', in V. Richardson (ed.) *Constructivist Teacher Education: Building New Understandings*, London: Falmer.

Meudell, P., Mayes, A. and Neary, D. (1980) 'Orienting task effects on the recognition of humorous pictures in amnesic and normal subjects', *Journal of Clinical Neuropsychology* 2: 75–88.

Mezirow, J. (1991) *Transformative Dimensions of Adult Learning*, San Francisco CA: Jossey-Bass.

Neisser, U. (1976) *Cognition and Reality*, San Francisco: W.H. Freeman.

Novak, J.D. (1990) 'Concept mapping: a useful tool for science education', *Journal of Research in Science Teaching* 10: 937–49.

Novak, J.D. and Godwin, D.B. (1984) *Learning How to Learn*, Cambridge, Mass.: Cambridge University Press.

Okebukola, P.A. (1992) 'Can good concept mappers be good problem solvers in science?' *Educational Psychology* 12: 113–29.

Olson, D.R. (1970) *Cognitive development: The child's acquisition of diagonality*, New York: Academic Press.

Peper, R.J. and Meyer, R.E. (1986) 'Generative effects of note-taking during science lectures', *Journal of Educational Psychology* 78: 34–8.

Piaget, J. (1980) 'Language and Cognition', in M. Piattelli-Palmatini (ed.) *Language and Learning: The Debate between Jean Piaget and Noam Chomsky*, Cambridge, Mass.: Harvard University Press.

Popper, K.R. (1969) *Conjectures and Refutations*, London: Routledge and Kegan Paul.

Ramsden, P. (1992) *Learning to Teach in Higher Education*, London: Routledge.

Ryan, M.P. (1984) 'Monitoring text comprehension: individual differences in epistemological standards', *Journal of Educational Psychology* 76: 248–58.

Schifter, D. and Simon, M. (1992) 'Assessing teachers' development of a constructivist view of mathematics learning', *Teaching and Teacher Education* 8, 2: 187–97.

Sherman, L. (1978) 'Three dimensional art media and the preschool child', *Presentations in Art Education Research* 1: 97–107.

Svensson, L. (1977) 'On qualitative differences in learning. III. Study skill and learning', *British Journal of Educational Psychology* 47: 233–43.

Svensson, L. (1984) 'Skill in learning', in F. Marton, D. Hounsell and N. Entwistle (eds) *The Experience of Learning*, Edinburgh: Scottish Academic Press.

Thomas, G. (1997) 'What's the use of theory?' *Harvard Educational Review* 67, 1: 75–104.

Van Meter, P., Yokoi, L. and Pressley, M. (1994) 'College students' theory of note-taking derived from their perceptions of note-taking', *Journal of Educational Psychology* 86: 323–38.

Vygotsky, L.S. (1962) *Thought and Language*, Cambridge, Mass.: M.I.T. Press.

Vygotsky, L.S. (1978) *Mind in Society: The Development of Higher Psychological Processes*, Cambridge, Mass.: Harvard University Press.

White, R.T. (1988) *Learning Science*, Oxford: Blackwell.

White, R.T. and Gunstone, R. (1992) *Probing Understanding*, London: Falmer.

Zechmeister, E.B. and Johnson, J.E. (1992) *Critical Thinking: A Functional Approach*, Pacific Grove: Brooks/Cole Publishing Company.

2 Getting to know yourself as a learner

Diana Coben

What is learning?

According to the American educationalist, David Kolb (1984), 'Learning is the process whereby knowledge is created through the transformation of experience.' There are, of course, other definitions – and considerable debate about the nature of learning in adulthood (see Tennant 1997 for a fuller discussion), but this is the working definition adopted here. This notion of learning puts you, the learner, in the driving seat. It emphasises that, as a learner, you are actively transforming your experience, hence Kolb refers to this kind of learning as 'experiential'. It considers learning as a process in which knowledge is continuously created and recreated by you, the learner, rather than seeing it as something independent of you that has to be transmitted to you and that you have to acquire. It treats you as an adult, able to decide for yourself which approaches to learning suit you best.

As a student teacher or someone returning to study, you will have to deal with increasingly complex, and sometimes stressful, working and studying environments – the university, the school classroom, the library or information centre, the internet – all of which require a range of qualities, knowledge and abilities. This chapter starts from the premise that most people's knowledge and their ability to apply that knowledge in different situations is patchy, and that we all learn best when what we learn relates directly to our perceived needs.

Getting to know yourself as a learner and becoming a skilled and effective learner are aspects of becoming a reflective practitioner, a concept developed by Donald Schön in his book, *Educating the Reflective Practitioner* (1989) which has become influential in many professional fields. Teaching is a profession in which practitioners are more and more expected to reflect on their practice and in which preparation for teaching, on-course, is intersected with practice in the classroom. Once you become a qualified teacher, you will be expected to continue to learn and to develop – to become a reflective practitioner, in Schön's terms.

Principles of adult learning

It may be helpful to begin by looking briefly at the principles of adult learning identified by researchers as follows:

- adults learn throughout their lives;
- adults are often motivated to learn by the changes they are going through in their lives;
- adults learn in different ways, at different times, for different purposes;
- as a rule, however, adults like their learning activities to be problem-centred and meaningful to their situation in life, and they want to apply their learning straight away;
- adults' past experiences affect their current learning, sometimes serving as an enhancement, sometimes as a hindrance;
- effective learning is linked to an adult's concept of himself or herself as a learner;
- adults tend to be self-directed in their learning.

(adapted from Brookfield 1986: 31)

If you recognise yourself somewhere in these 'principles of adult learning' you are probably already on the way to becoming a skilled and effective learner. If you don't, don't despair – this chapter is designed to help you to get to know yourself as a learner, to maximise your strengths and minimise any weaknesses.

So what is a skilled learner? In her research on helping adults to become better learners in relation to their work, Sylvia Downs (1993) found that skilled learners tended to use a greater number of learning methods than less skilled learners and chose a method of learning appropriate to the type of material to be learned. Poor learners, by contrast, tended to be passive and put the responsibility for learning on to others; they tended to have few and often inappropriate strategies for learning. She came to the conclusion that 'People do not have to be trained in order to learn. People often learn in spite of the training they receive' – but that they can be helped to develop learning skills (Downs 1993: 207).

And an effective learner? An effective learner is one who learns at an appropriate depth, retains what they have learned for an appropriate period of time and can utilise what they have learned as required. For example, it may be sufficient to commit a telephone number to your short-term memory if there is only a short interlude between finding out the number and making the telephone call – this is an example of surface learning and short-term retention. Deep learning and longer-term retention would be appropriate for matters of greater complexity and significance in the longer term, such as much of the learning required in training to become a teacher. And, of course, learning is wasted if you can't utilise what you have learned as required.

This chapter seeks to help you to become a skilled and effective learner – to build on your strengths and make the most of your opportunities to learn so that you are free to concentrate on developing as a good teacher rather than worrying about your lack of study skills. By the end of the chapter you should have strategies in place to help you to learn effectively under pressure.

Getting to know yourself as a learner

Reflecting on a learning event

Start by reflecting on your current or recent experience as a learner – preferably not on a formal course of study. Perhaps you are learning a language, learning to drive or exploring the internet – think about the learning process involved in your chosen activity. Write an account of the process (concentrate on the process – how you learned – rather than on what you were trying to learn). It may help you to get started if you structure your writing around answers to these questions:

- Why did you decide to start learning your chosen activity?
- Did you learn alone or with others?
- What worked best – and why?
- What worked least well – and why?
- With hindsight, if you were starting again, what would you do differently?

It's a good idea to do this exercise more than once with completely different learning events in mind – including something that you found difficult to learn – and see if any common factors emerge. A variation on this exercise is to write your account without mentioning what it was you were trying to learn, then swap your piece of writing with a fellow-student and see if you can each work out what the other was trying to learn.

Writing your 'learning life history'

The American educationalist John Dewey stated in the 1930s that the quality and continuity of experiences constituted key factors in learning and human development (Dewey 1963), and many others have followed his lead since then. If Dewey and his followers are right, then our learning experiences shape our lives, including our future learning. How have your learning experiences shaped your life? What has helped you to learn and what has seemed to get in the way?

One way of getting to know yourself as a learner is to write your 'learning life history', highlighting the factors – positive or negative – that seem significant in terms of your development as a learner. This should help you to recognise factors that may be affecting your learning now, but of which you are unaware. It should also help you to understand the learning process better, something that will surely help you to develop as a teacher.

You can organise your writing in any way you like. One group of researchers in Finland, who were studying the meaning of learning in adults' lives, asked their interviewees about 'significant learning experiences' (Antikainen *et al.* 1994). These they defined as those learning experiences which appeared to guide the individual's life-course or to have changed or strengthened her or his identity. They found that people mentioned both clearly defined events and vaguer, cumulative experiences, such as the development of self-awareness. For some people, a significant learning experience seemed to have given them the strength to cope with future problems and further learning. Try to identify the significant learning experiences in your life as a basis for writing your learning life history.

But perhaps a health warning is in order here. As Mavis Aitchison and her colleagues point out in their reflections on their research into the life histories of mature students:

> who we are affects how we write. Our life history of experiences, encounters and opportunities, hopes, fears and disappointments, values, beliefs and allegiances, our personality, our anxieties and desires, the tensions and contradictions in our lives, all bear down on the point of the pen.
>
> (Aitchison *et al.* 1994: 5)

Writing your life history is one way of bringing these experiences out into the open – at least to yourself. However, you need to be aware that life history research – on yourself or other people – has the potential to stir up difficult or disturbing feelings and memories. If you find the exercise stressful, you may prefer not to continue, or to seek help from a friend or professional counsellor. Remember: you do not have to show your 'learning life history' to anyone unless you want to. You are in control – you decide what to write and whether you want anyone else to read what you have written.

Keeping a learning diary

Another way of getting to know yourself as a learner is to keep a 'learning diary', in which you can record:

- your thoughts and feelings about your learning;

- any points of information about the learning process;
- any study tips that you want to remember.

Your learning diary can take any form. You can use a 'proper' diary, an exercise book, loose-leaf ring binder or a wordprocessor. If you prefer, you can tape-record your diary, but don't forget to label the tapes if so. Whatever method you choose, you'll need to set aside time for your diary entries – choose a time that suits you and the pattern of your days. After a while you should notice that you are becoming more aware of yourself as a learner and noticing things that you might previously have missed. It may help to read some of the diaries written for the 'Diary of 1000 Adult Learners' project celebrating the European Year of Lifelong Learning and the 75th anniversary of NIACE, the national organisation for adult learning, in 1996. Here is an extract from one of the diaries. It's by Christine Luke, a student teacher living with her partner and two children in Somerset and studying at Bristol University:

> We are a very diverse group, educationally and socially, coming from a wide variety of backgrounds and several different nationalities; some with lots of work experience and life skills and others with different experiences. Initially this caused some problems with the group 'gelling' but we have always found that in times of crisis we are 'there' for each other and this has been my most compelling experience – camaraderie – working with and for other people in a similar situation all sharing the same problems and pressures and dealing with them together even though we have come from varying backgrounds.
>
> (cited in Coare and Thomson 1996: 21)

She goes on to describe the format of her course, on which most of the subject lectures are devised in such a way that they exemplify different methods of teaching. As a result, she says:

> we experience a wide range of different learning styles which have included … role-play, presentations, seminars, discussions, debates and being put under exam conditions to remember what it is like for a student under pressure. Overall, there has been much independent and self-supported study and I think this is because of the type of profession and subjects we have chosen to teach. My qualification will enable me to teach Economics, Information Technology and Business Education at GCSE, 'A' Level and GNVQ standard. All these subjects change practically on a daily basis so it is important to be self-motivated, committed and be able to work independently to keep ahead of the changes, and future pupils!
>
> (ibid.)

Whatever subjects you teach, you too will need to 'keep ahead of the changes, and future pupils'. Keeping a learning diary will enable you to chart your progress and learn more about yourself as a learner as you do so. It may seem like extra work, but students who have kept learning diaries find that they are able to draw on them in preparing profiles and action plans and monitoring their progress. Remember that becoming a skilled and effective learner entails more than just skills: you need to develop a positive attitude to learning. Keeping a learning diary should help you to develop good learning habits, and as you become more interested in learning you should find that your attitudes change, too.

You will find references to your learning diary throughout this chapter. Remember: you don't need to show it to anyone else unless you want to.

Finding a 'learning partner'

Writing your learning life history and keeping a learning diary are things which you can do alone. However, as Christine Luke says, camaraderie is an important part of the experience of being a student teacher. Most of us find it helps to share our experience, and this may be especially important at certain times on your course, such as your first teaching practice. Find a friend or fellow-student with whom you feel comfortable and ask them to be your 'learning partner', working through this book together. You will need to agree ground rules so that you know what you can expect of each other. Here are some ideas:

- Discuss how (and how often) you will 'meet' to compare notes – it doesn't have to be face-to-face – telephone or e-mail conversations can be very useful, especially if you have other commitments that make it hard to spend time together.
- Decide what sort of things you want to use your sessions for: for example, talking through your feelings about studying, talking over the situations you come across while studying, especially those which involve working under pressure, and sharing strategies for remaining calm, maximising your strengths and tackling study problems.
- Decide how confidential you want your discussions to be, including whether you will allow your partner to read your learning diary.

Identifying your strengths and weaknesses as a learner

It's often easier to see someone else's strong points than your own, so your first exercise with your learning partner might be to conduct an audit of your respective strengths and weaknesses as a learner, based on your learning life history and other writing. Alternatively, if you prefer, you can do this alone. Either way, decide how you want to set out your 'audit'. Some people find it helpful to draw up two columns headed 'strengths' and 'weaknesses', others use different coloured pens – use whatever works best for you. Record the results in your learning diary for future reference.

Then think of circumstances in which your strengths as a learner are particularly useful and of ways in which you can build on them. For example, if you are methodical you are probably patient and unflustered, with good attention to detail – all qualities which come into their own in the routine tasks required in teaching and in learning about teaching. A good memory is also very useful, especially if you can harness your memory to a good understanding of complex concepts. If you have a good intuitive grasp of issues but are less secure on factual details, learn to value your insights – and work on improving your memory.

Make the most of your strengths as a learner. Start thinking of yourself as someone who can study, rather than as someone who finds studying difficult. Difficult work is just the work you can't do – yet!

Now look back at your learning audit and for each 'weakness' think what you can do to overcome or compensate for it. For example, writing yourself notes can offset the worst effects of a poor memory. If you tend to be careless in your essay writing, train yourself to 'edit' your writing – allow time to check your work, preferably after you have put it aside for a while; you are more likely to notice any mistakes when you look at your work afresh. If, when you are reading books and articles on a subject in order to prepare an assignment, you feel lost in a welter of different points of view, perhaps you are not allowing yourself time to think through difficult or unfamiliar issues. If you tend to fall back on assertions or anecdote rather than reasoned argument, perhaps you are not reading widely enough, or listening to a sufficiently wide range of points of view. Don't panic if you recognise any of these weaknesses in yourself: think of a weakness as something to work on, rather than as a permanent feature.

Think about what you would do if you got low marks for a piece of written work. Do you:

- give up
- start again
- re-read your essay to see where you went wrong
- read some relevant books and articles
- talk the problem over with somebody else
- ask your tutor for advice
- take a break to clear your head
- blame the computer?

(adapted from Coben and Atere-Roberts, 1996: 9)

Some responses are clearly counter-productive: for example, blaming the computer may be satisfying in the short term but it doesn't help you to solve the problem and avoid it in future. It also puts you in Sylvia Downs' category of 'poor learner', one who attempts to shift the responsibility for his or her learning on to others – or, as in this case, on to an inanimate object. Cultivate an awareness of different types of mistake and of your responses and you will be able to spot them more easily and take appropriate action.

Above all, try to see any weaknesses you may have as part of the whole picture of you as a learner, rather than concentrating on them to the exclusion of all else, and think constructively of ways of overcoming or compensating for them wherever possible. And remember, you are not alone – you can discuss your strengths and weaknesses with your learning partner.

You also need to be aware that, as Sylvia Downs (1993: 210) points out, you may be able to influence some factors in the learning process more easily than others. For example, she highlights the learner's own learning skills, attitudes to learning and propensity to be distracted from the task in hand as factors which the learner can influence. Conversely, you may be less able to influence your aptitudes, interest in the subject and environmental factors, such as the equipment and materials available to support your learning and any disruptions. Rather than seeing any obstacles as insuperable, a motivated learner asks, 'How shall I overcome any obstacles in my way?'

Strategies for improving your learning

Reflecting on a recent learning event, writing your learning life history and keeping a learning diary are all activities designed to get you thinking about the place of learning in your life in a new way. They are first steps towards developing learning strategies and study skills that will stand you in good stead as you 'study to teach'.

The next step is to develop strategies for improving your learning. It is important to recognise that there is no single strategy that will always work for you in any circumstances – and something that works for you may not work for the next person. You need to develop a repertoire of learning skills that you can draw on and utilise as appropriate. But how do you know what to use when?

Sylvia Downs' research may be helpful here. She found that poor learners were often confused over the distinction between facts and concepts, but that they could be helped, through appropriate exercises, to increase the number of methods of learning available to them and to choose appropriately between them. She developed a simple model (Downs 1993: 209) to distinguish the different learning requirements of:

1 facts which need to be memorised;
2 concepts which need to be understood;
3 physical actions which need to be practised ('doing').

She then developed examples of learning strategies appropriate for each element of the resultant – wonderfully apposite – mnemonic, MUD (Downs 1993: 223–4), and these are briefly outlined in the chart below.

M Memorising is helped by:
- exercises which introduce different ways of memorising.

U Understanding is helped by:
- defining what it is you want to learn;
- knowing why you're learning the subject;
- anticipating difficulties – cause and effect, prevention and cure; looking at the subject from other viewpoints;
- comparing and contrasting what you want to learn with similar and dissimilar things with which you are familiar.

D Doing is helped by:
- assiduous practice.

Look back at your writing on a recent learning event and at your learning life history. Identify the different elements of MUD that you have engaged in your learning. Look at different learning activities and you will notice that the balance between the elements varies. For example, learning to ride a bicycle, for most people, involves rather more assiduous practice (D) than conceptual understanding (U); similarly, learning the way to a friend's home involves more memorising (M), and so on.

In terms of learning to teach, all three elements of MUD are important. If you compare notes with your learning partner, you may find that he or she is good at memorising facts (M), or getting right to the heart of a tricky concept (U). Perhaps you are particularly adept at learning which involves 'doing' (D), so that you find it easy to develop a new practical skill that others find difficult, or you may be good at organising your work, listening to what others have to say, or responding appropriately when a child seems to be having problems.

Whatever your strengths, it's important to build on them, while not neglecting the elements of MUD that you find more difficult. The aim is to become an all-round, flexible and effective learner, able to operate under pressure when required. The more areas of strength you develop, the better equipped you will be as a learner – and as a teacher, since teaching is a practical as well as an intellectual activity.

Studying under pressure

Teachers and other education professionals need to manage their time and stress levels as efficiently as possible in order to cope with the increasing complexity and volume of work involved in providing an efficient and accountable education service. If you are a student teacher, you also need to develop the ability to study under pressure in order to cope with the demands of your training and assessments, and to prepare for your future career. You may have other pressures – for example, financial worries, or difficulties over accommodation, or problems in your personal life or with your health – which can interfere with your ability to study effectively. If these other pressures are serious, it is important to seek help. If they are not serious, or if you are lucky enough not to have any real problems, you may still find it hard to concentrate on your studies or to meet course deadlines, or you may suffer from 'exam nerves'. This section is designed to help you to manage your time and stress levels in order to enable you to study under pressure.

Time management

Good management of time means making the best use of whatever time is available. The key to effective time management is planning and prioritising in relation to context. If you are a student, that means, for example, pacing yourself so that assignments are not left until the last minute and revision for an examination is planned well in advance. Planning and prioritising effectively ensures that while everything may not be done in the time available, that which has been identified as high priority is done; the rest is kept on the agenda for future action.

You must also be able to distinguish between what is important and what is urgent – these are not always the same thing. Priorities often conflict and you will need to make a judgement in each instance. You will also need to consider the 'opportunity cost' (that which would be lost) if something is not done. Ask yourself, 'What is the worst that could happen in this situation?'.

In his book *Effective Time Management*, John Adair sets out ten steps towards better time management (Adair 1988: 151):

- Develop a personal sense of time
- Identify long-term goals
- Make middle-term plans
- Plan the day

- Make best use of your time
- Organise office work
- Manage meetings
- Delegate effectively
- Make use of committed time
- Manage your health

Tick off the items on the list which apply to you – for instance, if you are a student you probably do not have anyone to whom you can delegate work and you may not be involved in meetings as such, but you can develop a personal sense of time, for example by keeping a record of your use of time over a period of a week in your learning diary and then reviewing your use of time. Note down each point which applies to you in your learning diary.

Now see if any of the items you have not ticked can be adapted to suit your circumstances. For example, you may not do any 'office work' as such, but perhaps you could organise your notes so as to make it easier to find topics and so make the best use of your time for study. Add the adapted items to your list. Are there any other items which you think should be added? If so, add these to the list – but don't make the list too long.

Look again at your list. Make a note beside each point of the circumstances in which it comes into play. For example, 'plan the day' could be something you choose to do each morning in the bathroom or on the bus, or you could set aside a few minutes at the end of each day to plan the next day. 'Make use of committed time' could mean identifying the best time to work in the library.

Try managing your time on this basis for a week and then review your progress in your learning diary, noting down and changing anything that didn't work out. Review your progress again after one month. If you're successful in improving your management of time, you should find you have more time to do the things you enjoy and that you enjoy life more now that you are able to pace yourself – you should notice a reduction in the amount of stress in your life. The next section looks at stress management.

Stress management

Teaching and studying for teaching can be very stressful, so does this mean that the health of all teachers and student teachers is at risk? The answer is 'yes' and 'no'. Stress is not a disease and can lead to improved performance when sustained for short periods. Stress becomes a problem and can lead to illness when it is repeated and prolonged. Stress is inherent in teaching, as in many other professions: it can't be avoided altogether, but it can be minimised and you can learn to manage it productively.

People experience and deal with the effects of stress in different ways, physically, emotionally and socially, and it is known that people with certain personality types suffer more from the effects of stress than others. It is also often easier to see the effects of stress on others and overlook the effects on yourself.

Becoming aware of the stress in your life is the key to developing coping mechanisms which enable you to meet the demands of your course and enjoy a balance between work and the rest of your life.

If you feel that the level of stress in your life is too high and you don't feel able to talk to a tutor, talk to your learning partner, or to your partner or a close friend. Often the relief of talking to someone is enough to put the problem into perspective. If not, then you may need to seek professional help from a counsellor.

Meanwhile, try doing a 'stress review'. First, jot down in your learning diary three things which have caused you stress recently. These might include, for example: a row with your partner; an accident; missing an important study deadline.

Now jot down what you could have done to alleviate the stress you felt in each instance. Could you have avoided the problem altogether – for example, by organising your time better so that you didn't miss the study deadline? Could you have minimised the damage – for example, by talking over a problem that led to a row with someone, after you'd both calmed down? Was there anything you could or should have done to avoid the problem or to deal with it once it had happened? If not, then allow yourself to accept that there are some things that you cannot change. In each case you can learn from your experience by reflecting on it in order to improve your future performance – and in so doing you will reduce stress.

Repeat your stress review after one week and one month. In the meantime: try to improve your general health through improved diet and exercise; develop ways of relaxing; make time for your nearest and dearest and for yourself. Look again at the section on time management – working under constant time pressure is very stressful and if you can improve your management of time you'll find that other things fall into place. Remember that stress in moderation can 'tone you up' – it's too much stress that does damage.

If all else fails and you feel hopelessly 'down', try asking yourself these questions, extracted from Meredeen's book, *Study for Survival and Success* (1988: 126):

- What evidence is there to support your negative thoughts? For example, are you really a total failure or have you just failed in one area?
- Are there any alternative explanations of the event that are not negative?
- How might someone else react in the same situation?
- How does negative thinking stop you from reaching your goals?
- Can you react differently?

Once you've done your best to alleviate the ill-effects of excessive stress and improve your management of time, you can look at ways of studying under pressure. The key here is to start from where you are and develop your strengths in order to minimise any weaknesses. You could do a 'studying stress review', similar to your general stress review (see above) but focusing particularly on the place of study in your life. You might find it helpful to look back at your learning life history at this point.

Jot down three things involving studying which have caused you stress recently. These might include, for example: making a presentation to a group of your fellow students on the basis of your coursework; preparing for an examination; your first teaching practice.

Now jot down what you could have done to alleviate the stress you felt in each instance – look at how you tackled the problem and what aids were available to you. Why did you choose to do it that way? In retrospect, could you have done it better using another method? Were you in too much of a hurry – could you have tackled the problem if you'd given yourself more time to think? Were you trying to study in an unsuitable environment (with distractions, a high level of noise, etc.)? Were you tired or tense? If so, look back at the sections on time and stress management and see if you could improve matters. Discuss the problem with your learning partner – what does she or he do in a similar situation? The aim is to try and get some distance from the problems that are causing you stress, to get them in perspective and to identify ways of overcoming them. You should then be able to achieve a relaxed and confident state of mind in which you can enjoy learning and enjoy life.

Conclusion

To sum up, skilled and effective learners can choose a method of learning appropriate to the type of material to be learned from the wide range of methods available to them. They can learn at an appropriate depth, retain what they have learned for an appropriate period of time, and utilise what they have learned as required; they also have strategies for managing their time and for dealing with excessive stress. Getting to know yourself as a learner may take time, but it should help you to learn better, not only on a particular course but throughout your professional life. It has to be time well spent.

Donald Schön writes of 'the varied topography of professional practice' where the 'high hard ground' of technical rationality overlooks the 'swampy lowland' of messy, confusing practice – real problems, which defy a technical solution. Schön's 'reflective practicum' aims to help students 'acquire the kinds of artistry essential to competence in the indeterminate zones of practice' – in other words, on the 'swampy lowland' of professional life (Schön 1989: 18). As a skilled and effective learner you should be better equipped to negotiate this 'swampy lowland' while keeping your head high – and your feet dry.

Note

In this chapter I draw on my research on adult learning, in particular my work with adults on their 'mathematics life histories' (see Coben and Thumpston 1996), and on my book, *Carefree Calculations for Healthcare Students*, written with Elizabeth Atere-Roberts (Coben and Atere-Roberts 1996).

References

Adair, J. (1988) *Effective Time Management: How to Save Time and Spend it Wisely*, London: Pan.

Aitchison, M., Ivanic, R. and Weldon, S. (1994) 'Writing and re-writing writer identity', in M. Hoar *et al.* (eds) *Life Histories and Learning: Language, the Self and Education. Papers from an Interdisciplinary Residential Conference at the University of Sussex, Brighton, UK, 19–21 September 1994*, London: Falmer/Centre for Continuing Education, University of Sussex, pp. 5–8.

Antikainen, A., Houtsonen, J., Huotelin, H. and Kauppila, J. (1994) in M. Hoar *et al.* (eds) *Life Histories and Learning: Language, the Self and Education. Papers from an Interdisciplinary Residential Conference at the University of Sussex, Brighton, UK, 19–21 September*, London: Falmer/Centre for Continuing Education, University of Sussex, pp. 20–3.

Brookfield, S.D. (1986) *Understanding and Facilitating Adult Learning: A Comprehensive Analysis of Principles and Effective Practices*, Buckingham: Open University Press.

Coare, P. and Thomson, A. (eds) (1996) *Through the Joy of Learning: Diary of 1000 Adult Learners*, Leicester: National Institute of Adult Continuing Education.

Coben, D. and Atere-Roberts, E. (1996) *Carefree Calculations for Healthcare Students*, London: Macmillan.

Coben, D. and Thumpston, G. (1996) 'Common sense, good sense and invisible mathematics', in T. Kjærgård, A. Kvamme and N. Lindén (eds), *Numeracy, Gender, Class, Race. Proceedings of the Third International Conference of Political Dimensions of Mathematics Education (PDME) III*, Landås, Norway: Caspar, 284–98.

Dewey, J. (1963) *Experience and Education*, London: Collier-Macmillan.

Downs, S. (1993) 'Developing learning skills in vocational learning', in M. Thorpe, R. Edwards and A. Hanson (eds), *Culture and Processes of Adult Learning*, London: Routledge in association with The Open University.

Kolb, David A. (1984) *Experiential Learning*, Englewood Cliffs, NJ: Prentice Hall.

Meredeen, S. (1988) *Study for Survival and Success: Guidenotes for College Students*, London: Paul Chapman.

Schön, D.A. (1989) *Educating the Reflective Practitioner: Towards a New Design for Teaching and Learning*, San Francisco: Jossey-Bass.

Tennant, M. (1997) *Psychology and Adult Learning*, second edition, London: Routledge.

3 Curriculum studies

Steve Herne

Introduction

First, what is the curriculum? The term has usually been used to name the total planned course of study or programme of an educational institution or, in the case of the National Curriculum, a nation. If we are going to 'study to teach', as the title of this book suggests, is there a recognised curriculum of study to which we can all aspire? To answer this question we can explore some of the key concepts by looking at the history of educational study and the development of 'curriculum studies'.

In the past fifty years or so, what is encompassed by educational studies in colleges and universities has developed considerably. They have drawn heavily on major disciplines – branches of learning and instruction – to provide insight and a theoretical basis for understanding the processes of teaching, learning and designing curricula. Three major 'contributory disciplines' have been philosophy, psychology and sociology. History also is drawn on to provide a context for current practice and proposed innovation. For instance, the historical development of the wide variety of school subjects in the English education system is explored in *Social Histories of the Secondary Curriculum* (Goodson 1985). Ivor Goodson writes of the need to 'further our sense of history about the curriculum' (ibid.: 1) and argues for a meeting of contemporary study and historical perspectives. School subjects are not static. Accounts by educational historians of their evolution over time can improve our knowledge of the school curriculum, aid analysis, inform and influence policy and practice (Goodson 1985: 6–7).

Disciplines are not monolithic, and particular branches, for example behavioural psychology or developmental psychology, can influence the understanding of education and the view we take of children. We might, for instance, see children as trainees to be rewarded or punished in order to mould their response to behavioural objectives. Alternatively we might see them as growing plants in a 'kindergarten' who need the educational equivalents of sunlight, water and rich soil to fulfil their potential. If education is seen from only one or a limited set of such viewpoints, there is a potential for distortion. An interdisciplinary approach of applied philosophy – curriculum studies – has evolved to examine the educational field in its own right as a complex, multifaceted field, and to provide rationales for the development of worthwhile educational activity. One of its most valuable achievements has been to offer contrasting 'models of curriculum'. A clear understanding of the role of curriculum studies and the contributory disciplines provided by this chapter will help the reader to focus and locate their own study in the educational field. The chapter is based on conceptual research into the nature, scope and definition of curriculum studies, including a selective literature review.

Three contributory disciplines: philosophy, psychology and sociology

If these form the basis of curriculum studies, then it is worth starting by exploring some definitions and key concepts which underlie the broad understanding of each discipline. We can also look at where particular branches of each discipline have particular relevance for those studying to teach.

Although most people will be familiar with the names of some of the great philosophers in the Western tradition, such as Socrates and Plato, philosophy as a discipline remains somewhat closed, perhaps because it is not studied in British schools. From time to time there are reports of its successful introduction into individual secondary and even primary schools' curricula. The international best-selling success of *Sophie's World. A Novel about the History of Philosophy* (Gaarder 1995) shows the potential interest people have in this area. Philosophy provides us with a store of thoughts on fundamental questions about life, experience, identity and moral behaviour. It also exemplifies critical processes of thinking which allow us to reflect, develop our ideas, explore values and make reasoned judgements and decisions.

Philosophy as a discipline was originally divided into three categories, the metaphysical, moral and natural, the latter being incorporated into what we now call science. The word has been used to name an identifiable set or system of ideas – 'a philosophy' – and there are other subsidiary meanings, such as 'being philosophical' – thoughtful, or resigned and accepting. Exploring the nature, source, scope and limits of human knowledge – 'epistemology' (from the Greek word *episteme*, knowledge) is of great importance to the teacher or educator. Theories developed will have an important influence on the choice of content in education and the manner in which teaching and learning are organised. It will be valuable for those studying to teach to develop a broad understanding of the two great philosophical traditions, rationalism and empiricism, as they have had a fundamental and contradictory influence on styles and approaches to education. They are explored further in Chapter 4, and a good introductory passage can be found in Kelly (1989: Chapter 2), or they can be approached entertainingly through Gaarder (1995).

Psychology has been traditionally used to name the general science of the human mind or soul. Early references have been made to the 'psychological unity called the mind' and psychological research has focused on developing understandings of the personal, inner world of human beings (Williams 1976). Psychology has had a long association with the area of the mind concerned with feeling, with the private and subjective, the individual sensibility – the affective, rather than reason, intellect or knowledge. Currently there are multiple branches of the discipline including cognitive, behavioural and developmental psychology, which are all important in educational studies. For instance, educators have relied on the insights provided by research into child development both to establish expected norms for educational progress and to identify potential for acceleration through an understanding of how children learn (Stenhouse 1975: 29).

Sociology is the name given to the science of society. It ranges across documenting and interpreting observed social experience (empirical investigation), interest in social processes and social theory, and social criticism. 'Society' is the general term for 'the body of institutions and relationships within which a relatively large group of people live' and 'the condition on which such institutions and relationships are formed' (Williams 1976: 291–6). By seeing society as an object, 'the objective sum of our relationships', it is possible to define and explore the relationship of the individual and society (ibid.). Schools and classrooms, teachers' centres and university education departments are all social institutions and spaces where learning takes place within social interaction. Tensions exist between the desire of the centralised democratic state to ensure effective 'social reproduction' – the selection and socialisation of young people for jobs, careers and roles in society – and the notion of a 'liberal education' – a vision of education as a disinterested preparation for life, the fulfilment of human potential, and the pursuit of knowledge for its own sake. An undergraduate teaching degree often incorporates both tendencies with the acquisition of vocational Qualified Teacher Status (QTS) tied to the study of a specialist subject for its own sake, at degree level.

The study of aspects of the three contributory disciplines can provide us with powerful frameworks for understanding knowledge, the individual and society, to bring to our work with children in classrooms. However, as already argued, they can, on their own, distort our vision of complex educational situations. Each discipline has its own perspective formed and maintained by its community of scholars with different concerns to those of the teacher or educator. Moreover, the disciplines provide us with hypotheses – provisional knowledge about things that bear on educational situations – but go too far if they make recommendations for educational practice. There is a need to integrate the insights and hypotheses provided by the disciplines with the experience of the classroom and to identify clearly the concerns of the teacher or educator. This richer, interactive understanding provides a much firmer basis for making educational judgements. It is to fulfil this role that curriculum studies has developed.

Curriculum studies

As Kelly's definition (Box 3.1) indicates, curriculum studies is an interdisciplinary academic field focusing on educational practice.

> **Box 3.1 What is curriculum studies?**
>
> A useful, broad – if lengthy – definition of curriculum studies is:
>
> > the result of attempts which have been made ... to generate research and a resultant body of understanding which might make possible the development of a properly rigorous and practically relevant theoretical underpinning of educational practice, which might bridge the gap between or fill the vacuum created by the theoretical researches of people working in other disciplines on one hand and the unchallenged assumptions and largely intuitive practices of some teachers on the other.
> >
> > (Kelly 1989: 6)

Douglas Barns (1982: Chapter 5) describes the early transition of the debate about what should be taught in schools into a subject of academic study. He cites an American contribution to the literature on the curriculum, Ralph Tyler's *Basic Principles of Curriculum and Instruction* (1949), as a very influential publication. We can take this as a convenient starting point for the development of curriculum studies as a recognisable entity. While Tyler's emphasis was on evaluation, the basic question about what should be included in a child's education was soon addressed, joined in more recent times by an interest in the way social and political factors shape the curriculum. Douglas Barnes (1982: Chapter 5) has more recently identified four areas of study which include and extend Tyler's emphasis:

1 the planning of courses,
2 the organising and justifying of the contents of the whole curriculum,

3 the analysis of the social contexts of curricula and the management of innovation, and
4 the description, analysis and evaluation of curricula.

Lawrence Stenhouse, one of the key figures in curriculum studies and the development of the 'Teacher as Researcher' movement, further identified the improvement of the practice of teaching as the essential aim of educational study. The study of the planned programme – the curriculum – together with teaching and children's learning are unifying focuses to which relevant aspects of the disciplines can contribute. He advocated that teachers cast themselves in the roles of learner and researcher in the classroom and that curriculum research and development ought to belong to the teacher and relate to their own experience in the classroom. Curricula could be trialled, tested and refined in the 'laboratory' of the classroom. This could be addressed as a teacher's personal research and development programme, progressively increasing understanding and consequently bettering teaching and learning (Stenhouse 1975: Chapter 10). The expectation placed on students in initial and postgraduate teacher education during teaching practice follows a similar, if embryonic, process of planning, delivery, documentation, evaluation and reflection, leading to further improved planning, delivery, and so on. The notions of the 'reflective practitioner' and 'action research' are both important aspects of this teacher-led curriculum development approach. The latter is explored in more depth in Chapter 9.

This emphasis on 'practitioner research' is not out of place with the current interest in teacher research. The government preoccupation with raising standards has taken a different course through the publication of league tables, target-setting, a centrally prescribed National Curriculum, homework guidelines, literacy and numeracy hours, and quality control through judgemental rather than advisory inspection (OFSTED). An important feature of curriculum studies is that it is a field that remains open to those actively engaged in education, including the individual classroom teacher. The partnerships developing between schools, universities and local education authorities through teacher education and continuing professional development also provide fertile ground for equal and complementary research relationships, drawing on – and contributing to – curriculum studies.

An Introduction to Curriculum Research and Development (Stenhouse 1975) was written as 'a book instead of a textbook' for curriculum study. Stenhouse believed that only someone who could combine practical experience of teaching, research and development in the curriculum with an extensive knowledge of the literature could write such a textbook. It remains, however, an excellent reference for the fundamental starting points in the curriculum debate for those studying at postgraduate and higher degree level. A.V. Kelly, who has written extensively within the field of curriculum studies, is more accessible for undergraduates. He emphasises the need for interdisciplinary approaches so that educational problems can be studied in their own right and not as philosophical problems, psychological or sociological phenomena (Kelly 1989: Chapter 1). He asserts that educators need to be prescriptive – to offer advice, plan programmes, take decisions – and that interdisciplinary curriculum studies can provide the possibility of a rigorous approach to curriculum evaluation, decision-making and judgement. He illustrates the dangers of distortion caused by the adoption of a narrow viewpoint of a discipline with the problems created by the establishment of the grammar, secondary modern and technical schools in Britain. The creation of the system, he argues, was based on a psychologist's view of intelligence. This was done without a philosophical analysis of the concept of intelligence or a sociological view of the potential implications of such a system, particularly for those not succeeding in gaining entry into the top tier of the tripartite system. He emphasises that it is the critical or value element which is of fundamental importance to the student of curriculum studies; that the concern is not only with the how of curriculum, the methodology, but much more with the why, the justification for chosen practices (Kelly 1991: 6).

Some argue that with the imposition of a National Curriculum there is little point in curriculum studies or debate, as the curriculum is already centrally prescribed. The debate, however, does go on, and it must be conducted at a rigorous and critical level. It is the kind of debate that curriculum studies endeavours to fuel and support. One constant in education now is change. Even the firm promise made by a Conservative government not to bring in more educational change for five years, on the publication and acceptance of the Dearing Report (Dearing 1994), was superseded as a new Labour government swept to power anxious to implement its own educational priorities. If change is continual, students, teachers and academics need to go beyond familiarity with current structures and prescriptions to become critical educators, capable of informed contribution to debate and articulate in advocating their own beliefs and values. Centrally directed change still goes through a process of public consultation, and much change is based on a model where a government-appointed quango, such as the Qualifications and Curriculum Authority (QCA), identifies existing good practice and then disseminates it through a variety of channels. The good and innovative practice must therefore exist in advance, in at least some locations, for this to succeed.

Finding your way around in curriculum studies

If you are responding to an assignment or have chosen an area for study or research, you have a wide choice of potential reference material within each of the complementary disciplines as well as a growing body of material within curriculum studies itself. It is important to be clear about what each of the disciplines can contribute and how they complement each other. Box 3.2 gives an example of the potential material available for an assignment or enquiry into 'child-centred' education. Undergraduate students or those returning to study may be unfamiliar with most of the references in the figure and, whatever the subject, will need to consult introductory texts first to get a feel for the area. You could consult general introductory books from your booklist, looking in the index for entries on the subject. Where more than one page is indicated, this usually means that the subject is dealt with specifically. Skim single-page references as well, to extract other useful material.

Box 3.2 Contributions of the disciplines to understanding 'child-centred' education

Philosophy

For an assignment or enquiry into child-centred education you may look to philosophy to explore the ideas which influenced its development. You could explore the eighteenth-century Enlightenment, 'the Age of Reason', with its new emphasis on the individual, human rights, rationality, cultural optimism and a return to nature. Or explore the writings of Jean-Jacques Rousseau and his romantic conception of childhood, and more broadly, one of the two great strands of Western philosophy – empiricism, with its emphasis on learning through experience.

Psychology

Taking a psychological approach it would be hard to avoid reference to figures such as Jean Piaget and Lev Vygotsky. Piaget's theories of cognitive development can also be approached through some of his more contemporary critics such as Margaret Donaldson (Donaldson 1978/1987). You could perhaps compare and contrast Piaget's ideas with those of Vygotsky, such as 'social constructivist' approaches or with the 'behaviourism' of Skinner.

Sociology

A sociological perspective could focus on the institutional, political and social histories of child-centred ideas and practices. Another sociological dimension would be revealed through an exploration of literature on the nature and conceptions of childhood.

Curriculum studies

Moving towards curriculum studies, one could look at social and educational histories to chart the implementation of child-centred ideas in schools. This could include their promotion in the Plowden Report (Central Advisory Council for Education 1967) with its fundamental influence in the British primary school system and the subsequent attacks on the approach. In curriculum studies itself, it would be possible to find educationally focused and interdisciplinary writing exploring the philosophy, policy and practice of child-centred education. This could include social-science-based classroom research or conceptual research – work exploring curriculum models – which would provide the approach with a strong theoretical underpinning or develop critiques and advocate other approaches.

Undergraduates embarking on a course of initial teacher education will be presented with reading lists, which can be of an intimidating length! It will be helpful to consider which discipline and branch of discipline each book or paper represents or whether it contains an interdisciplinary approach, and the level at which it is pitched, before deciding which will be the most interesting or valuable to you at your stage. Following up references to books or authors in sections you have found relevant is also a good strategy. Students starting courses are beginning to explore their field, and as they move through their course, assignments will provide them with opportunities to digest and organise material and find their own voice. Postgraduate students may be secure in their undergraduate degree subject, but perhaps are encountering the field of educational study for the first time, or returning to study after a break. You will need to quickly establish a broad understanding of the field and locate efficiently what is useful to you. If you are studying at MA or higher-degree level, you will need to read more widely and develop a good grasp of the fundamental concepts and procedures in the field you are studying.

The examples in Box 3.2 would provide material for a substantial piece of writing, while individual focuses or small clusters would support smaller-scale or more manageable enquiries. What becomes clear from this is how the disciplines offer different yet complementary insights that can support but not lead educational theorising. Curriculum studies goes further, by applying ideas from the disciplines to educational contexts, linking and integrating insights to solve educational problems or support educational hypotheses. These in turn can lead directly into policy formation, ideas for educational practice or critical evaluation of existing practice. Within this, the student or researcher can carefully develop their own preferences, beliefs and values through the process of critical reflection. You will be developing your own theory of teaching – your personal pedagogy.

Models of curriculum

As already stated, the term 'curriculum' refers to the total planned course of study of an educational institution. To identify parts of it we can use prefixes such as the 'art curriculum' or the 'nursery curriculum'. The term 'hidden curriculum' has been used for those things that children learn as a by-product of the way a school is planned and organised, such as attitudes and social and gender roles. Where consciously understood and planned for by teachers, this becomes part of the 'whole curriculum'. There is also a distinction between the formal (timetabled) and the informal curriculum (voluntary extra-curricular provision).

A planned curriculum implies an overall rationale with a theoretical, if not philosophical, basis. One of the great achievements of curriculum studies has been to identify several theoretical curriculum models identified in Box 3.3. Models are simplifications, whereas real curricula are often complex and idiosyncratic, reflecting their human development over time. For example, the oldest form of curriculum planning – identified as the content model – is simply an approach where what is to be studied is listed. However, each traditional subject in the curriculum has its own history and supporting community, often in lively debate with itself and with those outside. Listing what is to be studied can be contentious, as the continual debate over which texts should be included in the English curriculum illustrates. We can use curriculum models to analyse and evaluate educational systems and documentation. For instance, we can find lists of content, drawn from an understanding of traditional school subjects, in parts of the National Curriculum. The National Curriculum, however, also makes use of objectives – setting measurable targets – which is more characteristic of the objectives model. We should at least know the strengths and weaknesses of a system we are expected to implement. Evaluation of a curriculum model should be based on a critical consideration of how effectively it reflects our understanding of education, children and the quality of its procedures for planning, particularly when tested in practice. There was little understanding of the curriculum prior to the 1960s. Each of the models will be explored in turn, showing how they have established a number of different approaches to curriculum planning.

Box 3.3 Models of, or approaches to, curriculum planning

The content model

Planning is seen as the selection of appropriate subject-matter or content.

The objectives model

Planning is seen as an identification of aims and more specific objectives. Curriculum is a product and its 'delivery' is achieved through rational goal-setting.

The process model

Teaching and learning are viewed as complex processes about which we know a little, but our understanding must be regarded as hypothetical. Planning is seen as translating broad educational aims into principles of procedure which can guide us in selecting activities and in interacting with children.

The development model

A refinement of the process model, which advocates the use of the insights offered by developmental psychology to establish principles of procedure which identify developmental needs and promote learners' autonomy.

(Adapted from Stenhouse 1975 and Kelly 1989)

The traditional or content model of curriculum

The traditional way in which the curriculum has been planned is to identify bodies of knowledge defined as subjects or aspects of subjects that are deemed 'worthwhile' or useful to pass on. The emphasis is placed on the 'content' of education, and questions of methods and procedures are secondary. The aim is to 'transmit' the pre-selected content, and evaluation is concerned with the effectiveness of the transmission. This is still the predominant form of curriculum planning in schools and the National Curriculum, which, despite being framed in terms of attainment targets (objectives), adheres in the main to traditional subject boundaries and in many subjects defines content in detail through 'programmes of study'.

It is clear that any approach to curriculum planning must take account of knowledge existing in the public arena as 'public traditions', such as bodies of knowledge; arts; skills; languages; conventions; and values. School subjects may involve a number of these elements but can be identified with one or other dominant category. In 1975 Stenhouse identified mathematics, science, history, geography and social science as primarily bodies of knowledge; literature, music and visual art as arts; reading, writing, commercial subjects, domestic subjects, technical subjects and games as primarily concerned with skills or traditions of craft; and languages as skills but having a special status due to their history as 'disciplines of thought' (particularly in regard to Latin and Greek). Current extended lists may find a place for media studies and drama in the arts, and the National Curriculum includes two new subjects: design and technology and information technology. In Chapter 4, other approaches to organising knowledge are contrasted in more depth.

Philosophical views developed in the rationalist tradition see knowledge as timeless and objective truths embracing all human understanding, values, aesthetics, ethics, social, political and spiritual dimensions. It is a hierarchical view, where intellectual and abstract thinking is seen as more important than feeling or practical activity. It maintains, perhaps, an artificial separation between the mind and body. The second broad tradition of philosophical thought, empiricism, can be seen as a reaction to rationalism. A fundamental principle of this viewpoint is that no knowledge can come into the mind except through the senses, a position that was established by the founder of this branch of philosophy, John Locke. A child's mind is seen as a blank slate, empty of any information or concepts. Children acquire knowledge through experience, which they use as a basis for building hypotheses about the nature of the world they inhabit. This knowledge is, therefore, subject to ongoing testing and revision as the young mind develops explanations and gains control of the environment.

The choice of curriculum content based primarily on a selection from bodies of knowledge is problematic. Whatever the individual student's, teacher's or curriculum designer's own beliefs and value positions, an acceptance of the responsibility of planning for a plural and democratic society promotes the educational aim of developing children's ability to make personal choices above the beliefs or value positions of one particular individual or group in that society.

The objectives model

The use of objectives in education has a long history, but in the past teachers planning their work have not taken them very seriously. During the 1970s and 1980s this began to change, often as a result of pressures of accountability, the influence of Schools Council curriculum development projects and, later, the introduction of the National Curriculum. Objectives are often given different names, such as attainment targets, level statements, learning intentions, desirable outcomes, and so on, and there is much discussion about the degree of specificity and the difference between aims and objectives. The major characteristics of the objectives model are that intended pupil behaviour is pre-stated with as much clarity as possible, that content and methods are chosen in order to achieve the stated objective, and that assessment and evaluation equate success with the modification of student behaviour towards the intended outcome. The approach endeavours to be value-neutral, maintaining a 'scientific' stance. It has been criticised for leaving important questions about what is educationally worthwhile to the practitioner and for accepting knowledge as predetermined content to be transmitted to the student.

Advocates of the objectives approach propose the learning of basic skills before progressing to more complex combinations in hierarchical steps. Being clear and precise about what we want children to learn allows efficient and rational planning and preparation. Assessment and evaluation are clarified by allowing monitoring and comparison of attainment against pre-stated goals. However, the pre-specification of objectives can be seen to deny the autonomy of both the teacher and the student. This may complicate and distort what could be a continuous, dynamic interaction between them, leading in unforeseen directions. While performance may be efficiently achieved, learning basic skills out of the context of a rewarding and intrinsically worthwhile activity may well kill the motivation and enjoyment in the very activity the educational endeavour is aiming to promote. Practice using the objectives model has shown that objectives have a tendency to be continually modified once they are being used. Perhaps this bears out the view that educational activity is far more complex than even the most detailed specification of objectives allows for.

There are educational situations where the objectives approach does not apply logically. In subjects like music and the fine arts, where an individual response is seen by many as a prime concern, it would clearly be inappropriate to decide in advance what the outcomes should be. Conversely, it has been argued that 'linear' subjects like mathematics and science lend themselves to the objectives approach.

The process model

The third major model of curriculum, the process model, requires the formation of general aims followed by the establishment of 'principles of procedure'. This can be illustrated through Stenhouse's (1975) examination of the process model in practice. This focused on 'Man: a course of study' (MACOS), an American social science curriculum mainly for 10–12 year olds. The principles behind the project have been expressed as 'pedagogical aims' (Box 3.4).

Box 3.4 Bruner's 'pedagogical aims' (principles of procedure) from 'Man: a course of study' (MACOS), an American social science curriculum of the 1960s

1 To initiate and develop in youngsters a process of question-posing (the inquiry method.
2 To teach a research methodology where children can look for information to answer questions that they have raised and use the framework developed in the course (e.g. the concept of the life cycle) and apply it to new areas.
3 To help youngsters develop the ability to use a variety of first-hand sources as evidence from which to develop hypotheses and draw conclusions.
4 To conduct classroom discussions in which youngsters learn to listen to others as well as to express their own views.
5 To legitimise the search; that is, to give sanction and support to open-ended discussions where definitive answers to many questions are not found.
6 To encourage children to reflect on their own experiences.
7 To create a new role for the teacher, in which he [sic] becomes a resource rather than an authority.

(Hanley *et al.* 1970: 5)

Stenhouse identifies these as principles of procedure. The *Oxford English Dictionary* defines a principle as a 'fundamental truth as the basis for reasoning … [a] general law as to guide action'. A procedure is defined as a 'mode of performing [a] task'. These principles are a clear guide to the procedures of 'enquiry learning'. The students are at the centre of the enterprise. Knowledge is not being 'transmitted'; rather, students are presented with first-hand evidence and activities designed to encourage them to use their base of experience, ask questions, develop hypotheses and test these out in an open, collaborative context. This is the essence of 'active learning', where students are engaged in developing their own structures and frameworks of understanding in response to their experience.

It is characteristic of principles of procedure that they are often relatively short lists of broad statements which invite reflection and interpretation and are easy to internalise. Principles are deep structures that can provide guidance in a variety of specific situations and contexts. They can therefore be drawn upon to provide guidance in planning and in moment-to-moment unforeseen teaching situations and interaction with children. They are responsive to individually unique and complex educational situations in a way which preserves both the teacher's and the student's autonomy. They provide guidance for choice of content, conduct and response to children, without prescribing the outcomes of an educational endeavour. It is hard to find published criticism of this approach, perhaps because there is also little evidence of its formal adoption in education systems in Britain or abroad. Predictable criticisms may well centre round the power it invests in the judgement and quality of the teacher.

The developmental model

In a more recent refinement of the process model, Blenkin and Kelly (1987) placed an additional emphasis on the role of developmental psychology. The term 'developmental model' (Kelly 1989) was later introduced. This model places the individual child and their development at the centre of the educational endeavour. The view rejects the planning of curriculum according to the knowledge to be acquired or the needs of society, or in terms of behavioural change. Its view of children is of free, active, autonomous individuals, and its view of education is one that endeavours to promote each individual's human potential.

In the developmental model, principles of procedure can be distilled from the insights into the process of education offered by developmental psychology. What is understood about children's developmental needs at different stages of maturation will be very much part of planning. There is also a concern with an analysis of the learning process itself, the process by which an individual makes sense of, orders and acts on their own experience. As no two human beings are exactly alike or likely to have the same experience, this has to be an individual process. It will involve active learning and require strategies that are individually responsive rather than aimed at a uniform mass. The developmental view does not ascribe hierarchical values to different aspects of cognitive functioning. A holistic view is taken of human experience. The forms of development identified by developmental psychologists and the curriculum theorists promoting this approach include 'all the stages of cognitive functioning or command of the modes of representation ... all dimensions of human functioning – moral, social and affective as well as cognitive' (Kelly 1989: 108).

The developmental model is identified with, and shares much of the criticism aimed at, child-centred approaches to education. One motive for its evolution has been a desire to bring a strong analysis to the theoretical and procedural basis of the child-centred approach. The interdisciplinary approach of curriculum studies is well suited to providing this, as Box 3.5 indicates.

Developments in curriculum studies

Much literature, particularly in America, focuses on establishing broader 'conceptions' of curriculum, going further than 'models' of curriculum which centre on planning. These aim to identify major themes that could unify the diverse debates of curriculum theorists. An important five-part model emerged in the early 1970s in *Conflicting Conceptions of the Curriculum* (Eisner and Vallence 1973), in which our earlier discussion of models can be located. In Box 3.5 the five conceptions have been linked with the corresponding curriculum model (in brackets).

Box 3.5 Five conceptions of the curriculum

Curriculum as an **academic–rationalist** vehicle for transmission of civilisation's intellectual heritage (**content**).

Curriculum-making as a **technological** problem (**objectives**).

Curriculum as a means of enabling students to reach their full **self-actualised** potential (**process**).

Curriculum as a means of **developing cognitive processes** in children (**development**).

Curriculum as a **social–reconstructionalist** means of initiating social reform.

(Adapted from Eisner and Vallence 1973)

In a paper over a decade later, one of the authors (Vallence 1986) discusses changes brought about in her understanding and changes in the curriculum debate. The 'technological conception' – including both the objectives approach to planning and the added resources available to teaching and learning through the information communications technology revolution – is now seen as concerned with the 'means' of education. These are tools that can be used in conjunction with any of the other conceptions. They have neutral values and offer resources to all.

The 'social–reconstructionalist' conception, which she defines as a curriculum which aims to empower students to criticise and improve on society, has been affected by the swing from the social activism of the 1960s to the politics of the new right and social conservatism. Other strands have been picked up by new fundamentalism and a desire to refashion society along the lines of religious-based morality (ibid.). The 'self-actualisation' conception, which most closely relates to process model and child-centred rationales, has also been affected by social changes. If it survives at all in the current context, it is as an underlying principle concerned with sensitivity to children's individuality, personal learning plans and self-paced learning. She argues that the 'academic–rationalist perspective' (which most closely relates to the traditional or content model) is the most enduring perspective, with its practical translation into a subject-based curriculum. The 'cognitive-process' orientation which relates to the developmental model, is described as being concerned with the development of intellectual skills such as 'reasoning, analysis, criticism, problem solving, judgement, etc., using specific subject areas and content as vehicles of development' (ibid.). She believes this conception also still holds relevance. She concludes by identifying what she sees as a new conception focused on curriculum for personal success within highly competitive fields – subtly different to the self-actualisation perspective – and describes her own conception of a curriculum which aims to create in students a personal commitment to lifelong learning.

Elsewhere, the curriculum has been characterised by Zaret (1986) as a 'metaphor' for lives being lived in classrooms and schools, arguing that the way we conceptualise the curriculum will have a decisive impact on the kind of schools and lives we create. Zaret feels that curriculum metaphors are bogged down by measurement, with attempts to standardise and systemise, which puts at risk a concern with the human aspects of school institutions. She proposes a radical transformation of the way we think about and discuss educational activity – that 'a curriculum is created, acted upon and recreated when a particular group of people at a particular time in a particular school setting work and play together in fulfilling their emerging purposes and directions' (Zaret 1986: 47) – a phenomenological perspective.

King (1986) goes further in defining the curriculum as a contextualised social process, asserting that the curriculum is a 'situated event'. She draws an analogy with theatre – events in special settings taking place at a specific time. 'Most curricular events exist on a continuum between the contrived elegance of grand opera and the dramatic spontaneity of street theatre' (ibid.: 36). She points out that, unlike theatre, all must participate, attendance is required in formal settings, and the aim is education rather than entertainment! To be successful, educational events must be accomplished with sufficient 'daring and dazzle' to hold attention (ibid.). This fresh perspective implies that an understanding of a curriculum can only be gained by experiencing the classroom life of an 'event'. The event, however, is 'situated' in a number of interwoven contexts that provide structures and meaning. These are identified as the classroom context (teacher, books, materials, content, children); the personal and social context (each participant's previous experiences, present aptitudes, interests, skills and attitudes which together create the social context); the historical context (the influence of preceding events, sequences, curriculum policy, etc.); and the political context, including the social hierarchy present in the classroom and school, relationships of influence, authority and power and political and economic arrangements in the larger society (ibid.).

Summary

This chapter began by looking at three contributory disciplines – philosophy, psychology and sociology – and curriculum studies as an interdisciplinary academic field focusing on educational practice. An example of application to a child-centred educational theme showed how the perspectives of the disciplines and of curriculum studies itself could influence response to assignments or educational enquiries. The major curriculum planning models were reviewed, particularly the two more recent which have developed to replace the traditional content-based approach. Finally a number of more recent developments in the field of curriculum studies have been introduced, starting from the identification of five 'conceptions of the curriculum' in the 1970s and concluding with a perspective of the curriculum as a contextualised social process.

Acknowledgement

Many thanks to Gwyn Edwards, Lecturer in Curriculum Studies Department of Educational Studies, Goldsmiths College, University of London, for pointing me in the direction of the more recent developments in curriculum studies.

References

Barns, D. (1982) *Practical Curriculum Study*, London: Routledge.

Blenkin, G.M. and Kelly, A.V. (1987) *The Primary Curriculum: A Process Approach to Curriculum Planning*, London: Harper and Row.

Central Advisory Council for Education (1967) *Children and Their Primary Schools* (The Plowden Report), London: HMSO.

Dearing, R. (1994) *The National Curriculum and its Assessment: Final Report*, London: SCAA.

Donaldson, M. (1978/1987) *Children's Minds*, London: Fontana (both dates).

Eisner, E. and Vallence, E. (eds) (1973) *Conflicting Conceptions of the Curriculum*, Berkeley, CA: McCutchan.

Gaarder, J. (1995) *Sophie's World. A Novel about the History of Philosophy*, London: Phoenix House.

Goodson, I.F. (1985) *Social Histories of the Secondary Curriculum*, London: Falmer.

Hanley, J.P., Whitla, D.K., Moo, E.W. and Walter, A.S. (1970) *Curiosity, Competence, Community: Man, a Course of Study, an Evaluation*, Cambridge, Mass.: Educational Development Centre.

Kelly, A.V. (1989) *The Curriculum, Theory and Practice*, third edition, London: Paul Chapman.

King, N.R. (1986) 'Recontextualising the curriculum', *Theory into Practice* 25, 1: 36–40.

Schubert, W.H. (1994) 'Alternative curriculum designs', *Curriculum and Teaching* 9, 1: 26–31.

Stenhouse, L. (1975) *An Introduction to Curriculum Research and Development*, London: Heinemann.

Tyler, R. (1949) *Basic Principles of Curriculum and Instruction*, Chicago: University Press.

Vallence, E. (1986) 'A second look at conflicting conceptions of the curriculum', *Theory Into Practice* 25, 1: 24–30.

Williams, R. (1976) *Key Words. A Vocabulary of Culture and Society*, London: Fontana.

Zaret, E. (1986) 'The uncertainty principle in curriculum planning', *Theory into Practice* 25, 1: 46–52.

4 Developing subject knowledge

Barbara Allebone and Dan Davies

Introduction

What qualities, skills and abilities make an effective teacher? Educators know from experience that it is necessary to understand an area of learning in order to teach it well, but that understanding on its own is not enough. There are many other kinds of knowledge a teacher needs in order to be effective in the classroom. Throughout the last century educators such as Dewey (1904), Scheffler (1965) and Shulman (1987) have discussed and attempted to define and categorise the knowledge and understanding that teachers need. Shulman (1987: 8) has suggested the following categorisation:

- content knowledge;
- general pedagogical knowledge, with special reference to those broad principles and strategies of classroom management and organisation that appear to transcend subject matter;
- curriculum knowledge, with particular grasp of the materials and programmes that serve as 'tools of the trade' for teachers;
- pedagogical content knowledge, that special amalgam of content and pedagogy that is uniquely the province of teachers, their own special form of professional understanding;
- knowledge of learners and their characteristics;
- knowledge of educational contexts, ranging from the workings of the group or classroom, the governance and financing of school districts, to the character of communities and cultures; and
- knowledge of historical ends, purposes and values, and their philosophical and historical grounds.

Several of these areas of knowledge are particularly relevant to our purpose and worth exploring in more depth. However, before we do this it is necessary to stress the topicality of this issue. There has been increasing anxiety in UK government circles over recent years that teachers – particularly those in primary schools – have insufficient subject knowledge to deal with some areas of the curriculum. These concerns came into sharper focus with the introduction of the National Curriculum in England and Wales in 1990. They also resulted in the introduction of a National Curriculum for Initial Teacher Training (DfEE 1998a) which specified, in three sections:

- A Pedagogical knowledge and understanding required by trainees to secure pupils' progress
- B Effective teaching and assessment methods
- C Trainees' knowledge and understanding

(DfEE 1998a: 33)

These spheres of teachers' knowledge (particularly Section C) relate closely to some of the headings in Shulman's model, described above.

Content knowledge

We expect teachers to understand what they teach in a variety of different ways, to recognise the conceptual links within their content area and the relationship with other realms of learning. If such content is organised in terms of school 'subjects', we also expect teachers to possess some comprehension of the purpose for its inclusion within the curriculum, and how it may contribute to pupils' broader development.

However, it is worth noting that the demands on teachers to 'understand' their subjects are only present if the school curriculum is to be defined in terms of knowledge content to be transmitted to pupils. (It would be possible, for example, to define curriculum content purely in terms of the development of particular faculties and skills in the learner.) Furthermore, we cannot assume that the nature and status of this knowledge content is not open to question, simply because it is prescribed by some central authority. For example, the model of knowledge inherent in the National Curriculum could be seen as broadly 'rationalist' in nature. Rationalism was named after the ideas of the Greek philosopher Plato, who accorded certain forms of knowledge the status of 'transcendent', or incapable of question. The implication for teachers is that we need to learn this knowledge because it is 'true', and we must transmit it to pupils in the most effective way possible that they too may know 'the facts'. The National Curriculum also contains elements that may be considered 'empiricist' (deriving knowledge from direct observation of nature) which leads teachers to focus upon 'skills of enquiry' in subjects such as science and geography. The outcomes of such enquiry are seen as the acquisition by learners of 'objective' knowledge about 'reality', which further reinforces the emphasis on teachers' prior understanding of the 'facts' pupils will 'discover'.

If, on the other hand, we were to treat knowledge as uncertain and provisional, and the curriculum as a process of developing engagement with this shifting knowledge, a very different model of learning might be required on the part of teachers and pupils. We would then need to question and explore the knowledge presented to us, constructing our own meanings from it and encouraging children to do likewise. The purpose of teachers' subject understanding in such a 'constructivist' curriculum might be to explore pupils' existing ways of making sense of their world within a broad 'conceptual map' of powerful ideas from a variety of times and cultures.

We do not necessarily achieve this depth of understanding through studying subjects in school for formal tests and examinations. For example, research carried out by Askew *et al.* at King's College (1997) on effective teachers of numeracy found that being a highly effective teacher was not associated with having an A level or degree in mathematics, but rather was related to the teacher's beliefs and understandings in what it means to be numerate, of the relationship between teaching and learning and the teacher's strategies. Thus we can see that the acquisition of a broad understanding of content is inseparable from the development of general pedagogic knowledge – planning, organising, interacting, assessing, etc. – without which the former is useless.

Curriculum knowledge

It is difficult to find compelling ways of representing specific ideas or concepts in a subject area without considering the particular curriculum materials which exemplify the content. Where such a curriculum is centrally controlled, as in England and Wales, teachers must constantly update their knowledge of documentation and initiatives, such as National Literacy and Numeracy Strategies (DfEE 1998b, 1998c) which govern the ways in which this content is organised and 'delivered'. However, it cannot be assumed that what is in place is the only model of curriculum possible, or even that it will not change in the future. In particular, we as learners may find it easier to organise the knowledge we need in different ways more appropriate to our purposes of becoming effective teachers. The National Curriculum for Initial Teacher Training (DfEE 1998a) achieves this to a certain extent, but is still bound by traditional models of curriculum framed in terms of subject disciplines.

The traditional curriculum subject disciplines, within which we categorise our knowledge, are often accepted without question. We tend to assume that this is the 'logical' or 'natural' way to organise learning, without really asking where these subject boundaries came from. The work of Goodson (1994) and others has, in recent years, begun to question this assumption and to cast light on the origins of many of the school subjects we now take for granted. Goodson suggests that 'subjects are not monolithic entities but shifting amalgamations of subgroups and traditions which through contestation and compromise influence the direction of change' (ibid.: 42). He characterises the development of a subject within the school curriculum as a striving by subject associations and other interested parties for academic respectability. The recent emergence of technology as a discipline within the curricula of many countries is an example of this political manoeuvring, involving pressure from industry for vocational education and from teachers of traditional 'craft' subjects for greater status and recognition. So what we recognise as a 'subject' or legitimate form of knowledge will tend to change with time, and it may be valuable to look at other ways of classifying human intellectual pursuits.

An alternative to the traditional model inherent within the National Curriculum for England and Wales is an approach advocated by Her Majesty's Inspectorate (HMI 1985) which defines the curriculum in terms of nine 'areas of experience' (see Table 4.1, column 2). These areas appear at first glance to correspond to traditional subject titles, but actually encompass much broader educational aims: 'it is necessary to look through the subject or discipline to the areas of experience and knowledge to which it may provide access, and to the skills and attitudes which it may assist to develop' (DES 1977: 6). This approach represents, to an extent, the quest for a deeper structure and the rejection of socially created subject boundaries. In order to develop the depth of understanding we require as teachers, it is necessary to pursue this deeper structure.

The theory of multiple intelligences

One way of looking more deeply at curriculum may be provided by the model put forward by Gardner (1983), which sought to reflect a theory of mental structure in the organisation of knowledge domains. Gardner's suggestion that each person possesses not one but multiple intelligences makes the link between human learning and our categorisation of knowledge explicit. Gardner's theory, derived from studies of gifted individuals and neurobiological surveys of the brain, proposes a small number – 'maybe as few as seven' – of distinct forms of information processing which govern every area of human thought and action. As with the HMI model, at first sight (see Table 4.1) some of these intelligences may seem to correspond closely to traditional subject areas, but their significance, claims Gardner, goes much deeper than that: 'I believe that, at the core of each intelligence, there exists a computational capacity, or information-processing device, which is unique to that particular intelligence, and upon which are based

Table 4.1 Three ways of organising curriculum knowledge

'Traditional' subjects (Key Stages 1 and 2 of the National Curriculum, England: DfE 1995)	***Areas of experience*** (The Curriculum from 5 to 16: HMI 1985)	***Multiple intelligences*** (Gardner 1983)
English 'English should develop pupils' abilities to communicate effectively in speech and writing and to listen with understanding. It should also enable them to be enthusiastic and knowledgeable readers.'	**Linguistic and literary** 'Command of language in listening, speaking, reading and writing.'	**Linguistic intelligence** 'To the extent that language were to be considered a visual medium, it would flow much more directly into spatial forms of intelligence; that this is not the case is underscored by the fact that reading is invariably disturbed by injury to the language system, while, amazingly, this linguistic decoding capacity proves robust despite massive injury to the visual–spatial centres of the brain.'
Mathematics 'Sorting, classifying, making comparisons and searching for patterns should apply to work on number, shape and space, and handling data.'	**Mathematical** 'Appreciate relationships and pattern in both number and space.'	**Logical–mathematical** 'This form of thought can be traced to a confrontation with the world of objects ... the roots of the highest regions of logical, mathematical and scientific thought can be found in the simple actions of young children upon the physical objects in their worlds.'
Science 'Contexts derived from life processes and living things, materials and their properties and physical processes should be used to teach pupils about experimental and investigative methods.'	**Scientific** 'Knowledge and understanding of the natural world and the world as modified by human beings ... a process of enquiry.'	**Spatial intelligence** 'Central to spatial intelligence are the capacities to perceive the visual world accurately, to perform transformations and modifications upon one's initial perceptions, and to be able to re-create aspects of one's visual experience, even in the absence of relevant physical stimuli.'

'Traditional' subjects (Key Stages 1 and 2 of the National Curriculum, England: DfE 1995)	*Areas of experience* (The Curriculum from 5 to 16: HMI 1985)	*Multiple intelligences* (Gardner 1983)
Design and technology 'Designing and making skills ... mechanisms, structures, products and applications.'	**Technological** 'The essence of technology lies in the process of bringing about change or exercising control over the environment. This process is a particular form of problem solving ... It is common to all technologies including ... electronics.'	**Musical intelligence** 'Like language, music is a separate intellectual competence, one that is also not dependent upon physical objects in the world. As is the case with language, musical facility can be elaborated to a considerable degree simply through exploration and exploitation of the oral–aural channel.'
Information technology 'Communicating and handling information ... controlling, monitoring and modelling.'	**Human and social** 'This area is concerned with people and how they live, with their relationships with each other and with their environment, and how human action, now and in the past, has influenced events and conditions.'	**Bodily–kinaesthetic** 'Characteristic of such an intelligence is the ability to use one's body in highly differentiated and skilled ways, for expressive as well as goal-directed purposes.'
History 'Chronology ... historical knowledge ... interpretations ... enquiry ... organisation and communication.'	**Aesthetic and creative** 'The capacity to respond emotionally and intellectually to sensory experience ... Art, crafts ... music ... promote the development of the imagination and the creative use of media and materials.'	**Intrapersonal** 'Access to one's own feeling life.'
Geography 'Geographical skills ... places ... thematic study.'	**Physical** 'Control, co-ordination and mobility.	**Interpersonal** 'The ability to notice and make distinctions among other individuals.'

'Traditional' subjects (Key Stages 1 and 2 of the National Curriculum, England: DfE 1995)	*Areas of experience* (The Curriculum from 5 to 16: HMI 1985)	*Multiple intelligences* (Gardner 1983)
Art 'Investigating and making ... the work of artists, craftspeople and designers.'	**Moral** 'Moral actions and the principles which underlie them.'	
Music 'Performing and composing ... listening and appraising.'	**Spiritual** 'Feelings and convictions about the significance of human life and the world as a whole.'	
Physical education 'Games ... gymnastic activities ... dance.'		
Religious education (Statutory, though not defined by the National Curriculum.)		

the more complex realisations and embodiments of that intelligence' (Gardner 1983: 278).

Some significant disciplines within the traditional subject model (for example, science) are notable by their absence in Gardner's formulation. These, he claims, are not distinct intelligences on their own, but represent, in the case of science 'a combination of intelligences (linguistic, logical–mathematical, intrapersonal) that has hitherto not been utilised in this particular way' (ibid.: 363).

The other distinctive characteristic of the theory – relevant to the processes of teaching and learning – is the inclusion of the 'personal intelligences', which Gardner defines in the following terms:

> On the one side, there is the development of the internal aspects of a person. The core capacity at work here is access to one's own feeling life – one's range of affects or emotions: the capacity initially to effect discriminations among these feelings and, eventually, to label them, to enmesh them in symbolic codes, to draw upon them as a means of understanding and guiding one's behaviour ...The other personal intelligence turns outward, to other individuals. The core capacity here is the ability to notice and make distinc-

tions among other individuals and, in particular, among their moods, temperaments, motivations and intentions.

(Gardner 1983: 239)

The significance of this personal area of intelligence for our own development of understanding is considerable. Our ability to learn from others (the interpersonal) or to reflect upon what we have learnt (the intrapersonal) is fundamental to our success as a learner. This is true whether we see our learning in terms of traditional subject knowledge, or as developing our use of the other intelligences in Gardner's model. Thus, these intelligences become not just the objects of our learning (as in the other two ways of organising curriculum knowledge with which they are compared in Table 4.1) but also the means by which we learn – our learning style. This point is developed further in Chapter 5.

Pedagogical content knowledge

The key to distinguishing the knowledge base of teaching lies at the intersection of content and pedagogy, in the capacity of a teacher to transform the content knowledge they possess into forms that are pedagogically powerful and yet adaptive to the variations in ability and background presented by the students. Shulman (1987) calls this unique faculty 'pedagogical content knowledge'. This includes the skills and approaches to the topics taught in specific subject areas and powerful analogies to enable children to grasp the concepts and processes involved. Wilson (1975) suggests that teaching, in the sense of 'getting others to learn', includes knowledge of subject matter in a way that is most useful for pupils' learning. Teachers need to have 'a clear understanding of what it is to make progress in the subject – the type of reasoning involved, its logical structure, the marks of a "good historian" [scientist, mathematician, etc.] and so forth' (ibid.: 111). It is this that distinguishes a teacher from a non-teacher. Teachers must understand both content and purpose of what is to be taught, yet it is more than this – teachers must be able to transform the content knowledge as they understand it into forms to which their pupils, with their variety of abilities, interests and backgrounds, can relate. Teachers need to reason a way from their understanding of the subject matter into the minds and motivations of the learners. If we are able to keep the needs of our pupils in mind at all times when developing our own understanding, this will make our learning much more meaningful and enable us to relate it closely to our primary purpose: that of securing learning in others.

The importance of teachers' educational experiences and attitudes

However we define the knowledge we need to teach, our attitude towards aspects of that knowledge will be influenced by our own learning experiences. This will have a profound influence upon the success we experience in developing our understanding for teaching. Let us take the area of mathematics as an example. Mathematics is regarded by many teachers as a body of established knowledge and procedures – facts and rules. In many cases, this owes much to the ways in which they were taught the subject in school. For example, when learning to divide one fraction by another, they may have been taught to turn the second fraction 'upside down' and multiply, achieving a correct result without a clear understanding of why this works.

The above is a clear example of what Skemp (1989) refers to as 'instrumental understanding', in which there is no awareness of the overall relationship between successive stages and the final goal, so that the learner is dependent on outside guidance at each stage. This Skemp contrasts with 'relational understanding': building up a conceptual structure with which the learner can get from any starting point (provided it is within the learner's existing knowledge) to any finishing point (the answers). The way in which we learned mathematics (or indeed any subject) at school may have depended upon our particular goals at the time. For many people at school, the primary goal has been to achieve desired grades in tests and exams, and instrumental understanding may be sufficient for this end, while leaving us with the negative feelings of non-comprehension: 'Once attitudes have been formed they can be very persistent and difficult to change. Positive attitudes assist the learning of mathematics; negative attitudes not only inhibit learning but very often persist into adult life' (Cockcroft 1982: para. 243).

Although our attitudes towards particular areas of learning may be difficult to change, it is important that we acknowledge them to ourselves when embarking upon self-directed study in the subject concerned. The consequences of leaving these negative attitudes unacknowledged may be serious, in terms of both our own success at developing the understanding we need and our resulting confidence in the classroom. It is unsurprising that teachers often find their own negative attitudes to different subjects reflected by the pupils within their classes. Negative attitudes form part of the 'hidden curriculum' which children are quick to detect; and teachers who lack confidence in particular curriculum areas may develop 'coping strategies' (Harlen *et al.* 1995) which reduce the scope of learning experiences offered.

Constructing our own knowledge as teachers

We have seen in this chapter that our ability to learn what we need to teach depends on several factors, including the nature and structure of the knowledge concerned; its relationship with notions of curriculum and pedagogy; and our own prior learning experiences (see Figure 4.1). It is also fundamentally linked with the ways in which our pupils will learn, so it follows that the model of learning we apply to them we must also apply to ourselves. In Chapter 1 a constructivist model of learning was introduced which sees learners as actively constructing their own knowledge, based on the interaction between prior ideas and experiences with new evidence (at first hand, or from secondary sources) mediated by their use of language in a social context.

According to this view, teachers will construct meaning in particular situations in accordance with their individual conceptual and emotional biographies (Resnick 1987). Knowledge is constructed by the teacher, as by children, through an interaction of prior knowledge with current experience. This emphasises the importance of engaging in the teaching process as a means of learning and reflecting on that experience in order to develop the range of pedagogic content knowledge required. It also reminds us to keep talking, both with our pupils and with our fellow professionals, in order to share and develop understandings.

Elicitation

The process of constructing our own knowledge begins with 'elicitation' (CLIS 1987). This is a process of finding out what we know already, which may be approached in a variety of ways. One of these is to conduct an 'audit' of our knowledge (described in more detail in Chapter 5) either using a pre-specified set

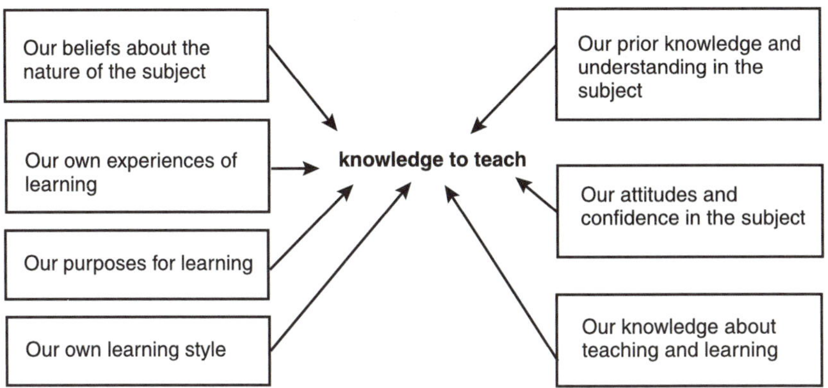

Figure 4.1 Factors influencing teachers' construction of subject knowledge

of criteria, or in the form of a brainstorm of everything we can remember about a particular topic. The form this will take depends fundamentally upon the area of learning concerned. Different disciplines require different intelligences and therefore different approaches. For example, in science or humanities it may be appropriate to draw a concept map (Novak and Godwin 1984) which is essentially a diagram of the relationships between ideas. Words or phrases relating to the topic under consideration are written, well spaced, on a blank sheet, and linking statements introduced with arrows to indicate relationships (see Figure 4.2).

In the case of mathematics, or disciplines such as visual arts, design and technology or music, a more appropriate approach may be to try out an example of a particular problem, technique or piece and evaluate the outcome. Was the performance of an acceptable standard? If not, try something easier in order to develop confidence and establish a realistic assessment of current levels of understanding or capability. This strategy of 'practising operations' is described in more detail in Chapter 5. For all disciplines, a useful diagnosis of gaps in understanding can be provided by attempting to explain the concept or technique involved at a level appropriate to the age of pupils taught; the act of simplification can reveal weaknesses of which we were previously unaware. The help of a 'critical friend' can be invaluable in this context, since they may be able to ask the questions which will probe our understanding and force us to clarify our ideas. This is the first step in a process constructivists describe as 'restructuring' (CLIS 1987).

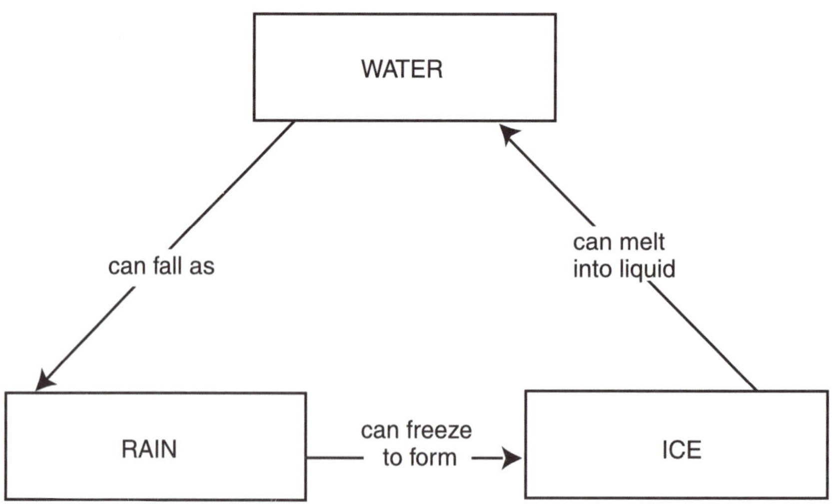

Figure 4.2 Example of a simple concept map

Restructuring and review

We now need to set about the process of clarifying, developing, supplementing and in some cases discarding our existing ideas. Again, there are many strategies for achieving this depending upon the subject discipline concerned, some of which are described in Chapter 5. For example, we may gain information from secondary sources such as books, video, CD-ROM or the internet which will supplement what we already know. However, we are unlikely to gain ownership of this learning and make it relevant to our purposes unless we engage in trying to explain it to others, test it against our prior understanding, or attempt to represent it to ourselves in a variety of ways (through drawings, words, pictures, sound, etc.). One way of approaching this process is to use a KWL grid (Know Want Learned) developed for pupil use by the Exeter Language Project as part of the National Literacy Strategy (DfEE 1998b) (see Table 4.2).

Table 4.2 Example of a KWL grid

What do I already KNOW about this topic? (elicitation)	*What do I WANT to know about this topic?* (restructuring)	*What have I LEARNED about this project?* (review)

Source: DfEE 1998b.

Referring to the middle column of the table, it is clearly important that we set an agenda for our learning, in order that we can review what has been achieved and compare with our starting point (the review process indicated in the right-hand column). However, as we have already seen, it is equally important that we establish why we need to develop our knowledge in a particular area, since this rationale provides essential guidance as to what we intend to learn (whether it be a discrete section of the National Curriculum for Initial Teacher Training or something much broader and in-depth) and how we will set about it. We hope we have begun to answer the why and what questions in Chapter 4. We will go on to consider how in more depth during Chapter 5.

Summary

Teaching is a complex and multi-faceted task. The teacher can take many roles – that of instructor, questioner, catalyst, facilitator, consultant, discipline provider, director, clarifier, setter of standards, setter of social climate, organiser, provider of resources, etc. The ways in which we learn to teach different subject areas will be influenced by our learning and teaching experiences, by the social context, current research and national requirements. The notion of 'good practice' is a construction determined by subjective views of the nature of knowledge, the purposes it is seen to address in society, and perceptions and beliefs about human nature and learning (Murphy and Scanlon 1994).

We need to move from personal comprehension of discrete subject content to preparing for the comprehension of others, which Shulman (1987) defines as the essence of the act of pedagogical reasoning, of teaching as thinking. We need to examine and analyse the factors that affect our knowledge base and personal comprehension, 'map out' what we need to learn, and then consider how we can best acquire the different forms of knowledge essential for teaching.

References

Askew, M., Brown, M., Rhodes, V., Johnson, D. and William, D. (1997) *Effective Teachers of Numeracy*, London: King's College London.

CLIS (1987) *Children's Learning in Science Project*, Information Leaflet, Centre for Studies in Science and Mathematics Education, University of Leeds.

Cockcroft, W.H. (1982) *Mathematics Counts*, London: HMSO.

Department for Education (DfE) (1995) *Key Stages 1 and 2 of the National Curriculum*, London: HMSO.

Department for Education and Employment (DfEE) (1998a) *Teaching: High Status, High Standards, Requirements for Courses of Initial Teacher Training*, Circular 4/98, London: DfEE.

Department for Education and Employment (DfEE) (1998b) *The National Literacy Strategy*, London: DfEE.

Department for Education and Employment (DfEE) (1998c) *The Implementation of the National Numeracy Strategy*, London: DfEE.

Department of Education and Science (DES) (1977) *The Curriculum 11–16*, London: HMSO.

Dewey, J. (1904) 'The relation of theory to practice in education', in C.A. McMurry (ed.) *The Relation of Theory to Practice in the Education of Teachers (Third Yearbook of the National Society for the Scientific Study of Education, Part 1)*, Bloomington Il.: Public School Publishing.

Gardner, H. (1983) *Frames of Mind: The Theory of Multiple Intelligences*, London: Heinemann.

Goodson, I.F. (1994) *Studying Curriculum*, Milton Keynes: Open University Press.

Harlen, W., Holroyd, C. and Byrne, M. (1995) *Confidence and Understanding in Teaching Science and Technology in Primary Schools*, Edinburgh: Scottish Council for Research in Education.

Her Majesty's Inspectorate (HMI) (1985) *The Curriculum from 5 to 16*, London: HMSO.

Murphy, P. (1997) *Making Sense of Science Study Guide*, Milton Keynes: Open University Press.

Murphy, P. and Scanlon, E. (1994) 'Perceptions of process and content in the science curriculum', in J. Bourne (ed.) *Thinking Through Primary Practice*, London: Routledge.

Novak, J.D. and Godwin, D.B. (1984) *Learning How to Learn*, Cambridge: Cambridge University Press.

Resnick, L.B. (1987) *Education and Learning to Think*, Washington DC: National Academic Press.

Scheffler, I. (1965) *Conditions of Knowledge: An Introduction to Epistemology and Education*, Chicago: University of Chicago Press.

Shulman, L.S (1987) 'Knowledge and teaching: foundations of the new reform', *Harvard Educational Review* 7, 1: 1–22.

Skemp, R. (1989) *Mathematics in the Primary School*, London: Routledge.

Wilson, J. (1975) *Education Theory and the Preparation of Teachers*, Windsor: NFER.

5 Strategies and case studies

Dan Davies and Barbara Allebone

Introduction: from styles to strategies

In Chapters 2 and 4 the wide variety of factors that can contribute towards successful development of the subject expertise needed for teaching have been outlined. It has been argued that we need to consider:

- the nature of the knowledge we require, and how it is organised;
- the ways in which that knowledge fits into our broader learning about the process of teaching;
- the specific demands of particular subject areas, and ways in which they are best approached;
- our own preferred learning styles.

How, then, are we to translate this complex network of requirements into a clear pathway for learning? The purpose of this chapter is to suggest a toolkit of learning strategies, arising from the authors' work with trainee teachers and colleagues on in-service courses. These strategies do not represent a total solution to the problem of acquiring subject knowledge, but a box of 'tools' from which we can select those which seem most appropriate for our situation.

'Wholes and parts'

Before we describe the contents of our toolkit, it is worth considering two further factors which may affect our selection of appropriate learning strategies. When considering how to acquire knowledge we need to be aware of the ways in which children will approach that knowledge when we come to teach it. Underpinning these 'preferred modes of learning' are what Riding and Cheema (1991) have described as cognitive styles: in other words, the ways in which we think. Riding and Cheema have defined cognitive style in terms of two broad scales: wholist–analytic ('wholes or parts') and imager–verbaliser ('pictures or words'). They have characterised particular styles of thinking at the extremes of these scales:

- Wholists tend to see a domain of knowledge as a whole, moving through it randomly but maintaining 'the big picture' in their minds, whereas
- Analysts tend to see knowledge in terms of a series of interconnected pieces, and move through it meticulously in a step-by-step fashion.
- Imagers prefer to work in pictures: they often represent knowledge diagrammatically in their 'mind's eye' and make use of drawing as a tool, whereas
- Verbalisers tend to express ideas in words: they discuss and think through problems verbally.

It is important to realise that cognitive styles represent 'sliding scales' rather than categories; they only express people's general preferences, but can be useful when considering how we might model our ideas. For example, in representing an aspect of scientific understanding, wholists who are also imagers would probably try to draw a large picture showing an overview of the area, whereas analytic verbalisers may be inclined to model the situation as a series of discrete 'bullet points'.

Another factor, which is of vital importance in selecting our learning strategies, is the purpose for our learning. At one level this may appear to be obvious: we want to learn in order to teach. But are we merely seeking after what Skemp (1989) calls instrumental understanding – 'brushing up' on our knowledge so we can teach it the next day – or do we require a deeper understanding which enables us to relate domains of knowledge to one another in our personal 'mental map'? The answer to this question will profoundly affect the approach we take to our learning process, which may be represented diagrammatically as in Figure 5.1.

The process outlined in Figure 5.1 is not necessarily as deliberate and linear as it might appear. For example, it is perfectly possible to set out aiming for instrumental understanding – 'I need to pass a test on fractions tomorrow' – and through the process of reading (distance learning) clarify a broad area of interconnected ideas concerning proportion, percentage and scale, some of which may not be directly related to mathematics or part of the immediate purpose for learning at the time. Equally, there is nothing to prevent someone who sees themselves as predominantly an 'imager' from learning collaboratively with others through verbal interaction.

The list of learning strategies identified in Figure 5.1 is not exclusive, neither is each a discrete approach. Any learning strategy may vary according to the context and may be developed accordingly (Riding and Cheema 1991). Learning experiences are composed of content, process and social climate, and we construct knowledge according to the situation and the purpose for learning. With this in

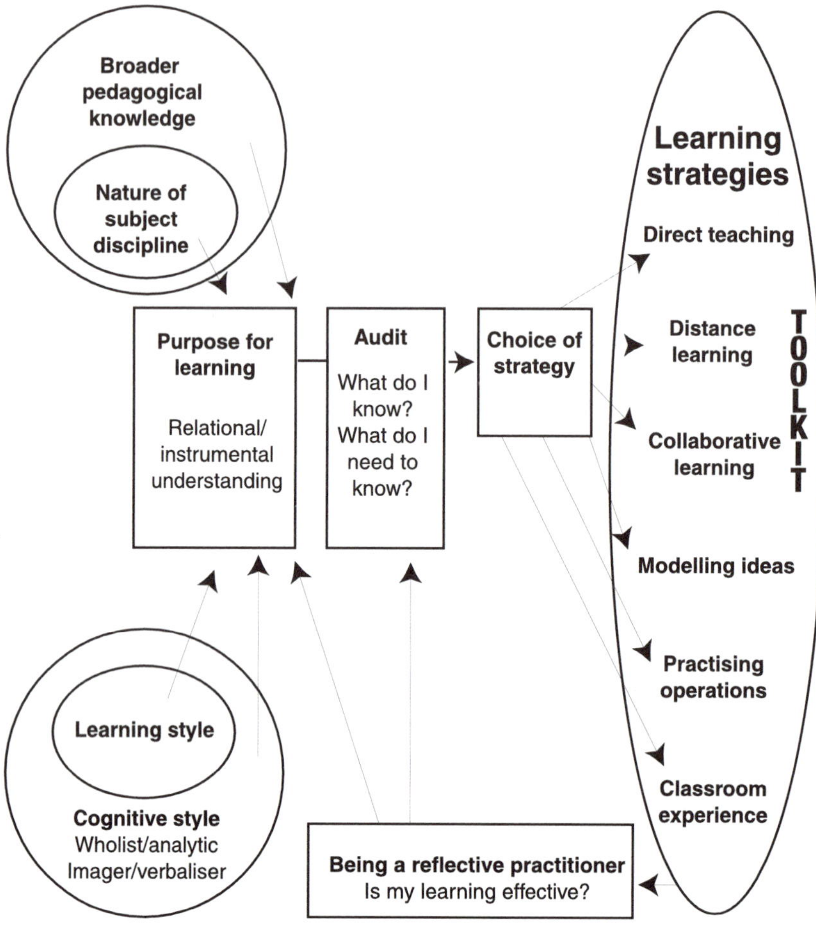

Figure 5.1 The process of selecting a learning strategy

mind, we will provide detailed guidance on the approach suggested above, and provide examples of what individual student teachers have said about their use of each strategy in relation to mathematical and scientific learning, to provide case-study exemplification of the process in action.

Auditing subject knowledge: defining the field of knowledge

When anyone sets out to learn something, they must first ascertain what it is they do know about the subject, and what they have yet to find out or fully understand. It is important to know just how wide the field is, and the boundaries beyond which learning is, at present, unnecessary. This process has come to be known as 'auditing', a financial term that is rather mechanistic to describe the complex thinking involved. The process of auditing can take a variety of forms according to the area of learning concerned. Different disciplines require different approaches: these might include evaluating existing knowledge against specific criteria, brainstorming or concept mapping (see Chapter 4) to identify and evaluate 'gaps' in knowledge and understanding. It is a requirement of the National Curriculum for Initial Teacher Training (DfEE 1998) that primary trainee teachers' knowledge and understanding in mathematics, English, science and ICT is audited against the content specified both within its own annexes and in the National Curriculum and that specified in the circular. Consequently, student teachers in England and Wales will become familiar with certain forms of auditing. Some BA(Ed.) primary student teachers at Goldsmiths found this a useful 'tool' in identifying the field of knowledge to be addressed:

> The maths audit was very helpful in identifying weaknesses. Defining the area made me more conscious of this weakness and highlighted the most important aspects.
>
> (student quote)

Others found completing the audit quite encouraging:

> I had begun the process with a better understanding of some of the aspects than I had first imagined.
>
> (student quote)

When asked to describe their levels of understanding and confidence in science – a subject notorious for low levels of confidence among primary teachers (Russell *et al.* 1994) – several BA(Ed.) primary students in Year 2 of their course experienced some difficulty. Some of the scientific language used in the audit instrument (based upon National Curriculum statements at Key Stage 3) was off-putting, and resulted in lower levels of confidence than students' underlying understanding might otherwise indicate:

> In fact, my knowledge was so poor I had no idea which questions to ask in order to improve it.
>
> (student quote)

The message here is clear: choose an auditing 'tool' carefully in order to build up confidence rather than destroy it. As a starting point, many courses provide an outline of intended content coverage, which can be expanded upon by reference to past exam papers or commercially produced revision guides appropriate to the level required. It may be better to start at a lower level than specified in order to refresh the memory from previous relevant learning experiences. This process may be effectively linked to the learning strategy of 'practising operations' (see below) since many revision guides and textbooks contain 'worked examples' which are useful for highlighting areas of misunderstanding:

> In order to start, I decided to carry out a summative assessment of what I knew already by completing a 'quick test'.
>
> (student quote)

Paradoxically, the process of auditing or self-testing can itself become a learning strategy:

> Focusing attention on the problem made the problem more explicit. I had a clearer idea about what I wanted to find out. This was useful because, having an 'instrumental' understanding, I was not even aware a problem existed (I could provide an answer without understanding the mathematics involved). So by increasing my level of awareness my knowledge and understanding had also developed.
>
> (student quote)

> While the main intention of these tests was to assess my own subject knowledge, unexpectedly this also developed my understanding. Of course, this meant that the record I made of my initial understanding was distorted by what I learned undertaking it!
>
> (student quote)

The 'tools' in the learning strategies 'kit'

Direct teaching

The most obvious strategy to try first is that of actually attending the course lectures, workshops and seminars in order to learn directly from a tutor. This is the more formal side of 'direct teaching', which may also involve asking a friend, relative or 'knowledgeable other' to help us in our learning. For many people, this may be the most effective mode of learning, because it involves an element of interaction: we can ask about what we don't understand, which is not possible in most forms of distance learning:

> I had tried distance learning before the session to see if I could go into the lesson with some knowledge on forces, but was still not really clear on any of

> my points of weakness. However, I found the direct teaching invaluable. There was someone there explaining each point and demonstrating how the forces worked.
>
> (student quote)

> I needed first to decide what areas of algebra I required development in. I then looked for a strategy to put into place which would assist my learning. Direct teaching was used whenever possible. I could take notes, ask questions and discuss with others.
>
> (student quote)

However, direct teaching is highly dependent on the effectiveness of the teacher, the relationship between teacher and students, and the time available. Defining what is meant by 'effective teaching' in such a way that all would agree is not a simple matter. Doyle (1978) observed that reviewers of research into teacher effectiveness concluded, with remarkable regularity, that 'few consistent relationships between teacher variables and effectiveness can be established'. An experiment at the University of Michigan illustrates some of the difficulties within the debate. Guetzkow *et al.* (1954) divided first-year students on a psychology course into three groups. The first group was given a formal lecture course with regular tests while the other groups took part in tutorials and discussion. At the end of the course, the lecture group not only outperformed the other groups on the final examinations but rated their course more favourably. However, the students in the discussion groups scored significantly higher than those in the lecture group on a measure of interest in psychology. Three years later, not one student in the lecture group had chosen to study the subject further, but fourteen members of the two discussion and tutorial groups had chosen to major in psychology.

Whatever methods of teaching are used, if there is a larger volume of content than time will allow, or if students are at widely different levels of understanding, the input received may not all be of direct personal relevance or sufficiency. It can also be argued that being 'told' something is a notoriously inefficient mode of learning and needs to be supplemented by discussion, visual material and 'hands-on' activities. These may well form part of the course, but if not can be undertaken away from the session as part of one of the other strategies (collaborative learning, modelling ideas and practising operations). Thus direct teaching on its own is rarely enough.

Distance learning

The term 'distance learning' is used to describe a wide variety of learning strategies making use of different media, whose common feature is the separation of teacher and student. In the most obvious example – a book – the 'teacher' or author may not even be aware that their words are being used as a learning resource. Much work in the development of effective distance learning materials has been carried out by the Open University over the past thirty years. This research has revealed the importance of learners 'constructing their own knowledge' through interaction with texts and other learners: 'From a constructivist perspective on learning, a vital issue in developing instructional practices for distance learning is the importance of providing opportunities for dialogue and for collaborative working' (Ross and Scanlon 1995: 38). So distance learning is immediately associated with another of our strategies: 'collaborative learning'. Ross and Scanlon go on to outline the pros and cons of various media for learning, particularly in the area of science.

Print

Students have control over the learning process, by either skimming text or working through it carefully. The text can be 'dipped into' at a later date to revise conceptual understanding. Print is not interactive; it does not enable debate (although it may represent it). Some specialist language or symbols may not be accessible to the learner, and there is no one to ask.

Finding materials at an appropriate level can be critical. Among the BA (Ed.) Year 2 primary student teachers at Goldsmiths, several have found it helpful to start their reading at an elementary or primary school level, or use a mathematics dictionary designed for primary children. This can enable students to explain the concepts in children's language before taking them to increasing levels of complexity and abstraction. However, there can be pitfalls in this approach, since the explanations offered in more advanced texts can seem to contradict the 'simplified version', as in this example:

> Rather than supporting and scaffolding I had become confused by trying to concentrate my learning at too much of an elementary level.
>
> (student quote)

Fortunately, with the assistance of a good library, there is generally available a wide variety of levels of text on most subjects, which need to be selected from carefully.

Illustrations

Pictures and diagrams can aid visualisation of complex concepts, help with the organisation of ideas and interpret or clarify or explain difficult text. For a non-'visualiser', pictures can confuse an issue. They are at best abstractions from reality – or misleading over-simplifications – and as such cannot be taken too 'literally'.

Television and video

The early use of television by the Open University was a form of 'distance lecturing' which had some of the advantages of direct teaching, but without any form of interaction. Students lacked control over the medium: they had to view it all at once and did not have the opportunity to study aspects in depth. Many of these disadvantages can be overcome through the use of video, which permits active engagement and student control through the use of stop and start, pause and review. Both television and video can provide vicarious experience of situations or phenomena which are difficult to represent in the classroom or a book (for example, a journey through space) and are well suited for representing visually or conceptually dense information (through, for example, time-lapse or slow motion). When used in a group setting, video often provides a good trigger for joint discussion of the issues raised, and if viewed selectively can provide a powerful learning tool:

> When watching a video you have the text plus the narrative. The two are usually closely connected. This helps my knowledge and understanding as it is visually stimulating, more real and easier to relate to ... Video increased my memory as I could see the connection clearly between narrative and diagram ... With the video I was able to follow the whole process compared to books from which I could not gain a full picture.
>
> (student quote)

Computers

Good-quality multimedia resources, used on a fast and powerful computer, can have many of the advantages of video, including access to 'real world' imagery, text, graphics, photographs, animations, sound and motion. In addition, there is the powerful extra dimension of interactivity: the ability to question the information presented and manipulate it in a variety of ways. The most commonly available forms of multimedia vary enormously in the extent to which they are interactive. Most contain elements of hypertext links between one part of a body of information and another. They can permit learning to be a process of discovery, involving 'browsing', taking notes electronically and 'capturing' images for use in representing our ideas and concepts (see 'Modelling ideas' below). At its best, multimedia can be a vibrant and exciting learning resource:

> The moving images of the solar system … represented the three-dimensional nature of the universe much more clearly than any two-dimensional printed image could possibly do.
>
> (student quote)

Content-free software such as the primary computer 'language' LOGO and spreadsheets have been found to be a useful resource by some students. Others preferred to 'browse' through software designed for classroom use with a purpose in mind:

> I found LOGO a useful program in revising my understanding of angles.
>
> (student quote)

> I suppose the strategy I used most was just working through various programs by myself and learning as I went. I think of a classroom activity and try and work it out, thinking of how I could fit it into the curriculum for children in the juniors.
>
> (student quote)

Most CD-ROMs remain expensive and require high-quality equipment to fully exploit their potential. In spite of their reputation for interactivity, many such resources promote a rather inflexible approach to learning, presenting knowledge as a series of 'facts' couched in highly technical, often inaccessible, language. It can be very difficult to find a particular piece of information, and there is the constant danger of becoming side-tracked or 'lost' in the huge volume of data available. This can be an even greater problem when using the internet, another example of multimedia which needs to be searched with single-minded diligence in order to find out what we actually need to know. Students at Goldsmiths College found it invaluable to have a list of questions to structure their enquiry, and frequently reported frustration at their inability to access relevant learning material.

Collaborative learning

Although distance learning in its various forms can provide a powerful tool, it is important not to neglect the social dimension of learning, emphasised by

Vygotsky (1978) and others. Through our discussions with fellow learners we 'try out' our ideas, receive feedback and hence modify these ideas, listen to the understandings of others and jointly try to make sense of a new area of knowledge.

> Collaboration with colleagues to discuss 'why' our results were so was fascinating and extremely helpful.
>
> (student quote)

This can be a very enjoyable form of learning, which in itself can be an indication of effectiveness but needs to be managed in a disciplined way to achieve results. Some Goldsmiths students reported disappointment at the outcomes, despite the evident appeal of this strategy. Their objectives for the discussions had been too broad, and students had come with personal agendas:

> I was surprised that my learning of the subject matter involved here was not really helped by this strategy.
>
> (student quote)

There can also be the danger of students reinforcing each other's erroneous ideas, so the strategy was generally regarded as a means of deepening existing understandings developed by other means:

> We used this mode of working mainly to consolidate and reinforce ideas and for us to probe our understandings and to assess their completeness.
>
> (student quote)

The lessons to be learnt from this experience are:

- set a clear agenda for the discussion or have a clear focus;
- ensure that the relevant distance learning has taken place beforehand;
- appoint a 'chair' to enable the process to remain focused;
- take notes and refer back to distance learning materials afterwards to check accuracy.

Modelling ideas

The act of modelling, or 'representing our ideas', is obviously not a strategy that can be used on its own: we need some external stimulus to provide us with something to work on. So having attended a lecture, read a book, watched a video or taken part in a discussion, we need to 'embed' the learning within our existing mental structures. There are many types of model, from the abstract or symbolic mathematical models of situations through to concrete three-dimensional representations in card or clay.

> One strategy I used was 'mind mapping' which is based on 'modelling ideas'. It uses a system similar to brainstorms, with a word in the middle relating to the area to be covered. Then each branch is a different colour and is about a topic. You use pictures and single words only. You look over this colourful mind map for five minutes … It really does work.
>
> (student quote)

The concept mapping technique described by the student (and under 'Auditing') is a form of mental modelling; the type of model which is helpful in any particular circumstance will depend on the structure of the knowledge presented and the preferred cognitive style of the student:

> For me personally I find modelling, in this instance drawing out the particular diagrams and layouts I'm trying to develop, works far more effectively than merely being given a 'handout'. I find the act of using pen and paper to physically record tends to embed the knowledge in a more concrete fashion.
>
> (student quote)

The student above is a clear example of a 'visualiser' (Riding and Cheema 1991). However, even for 'verbalisers' the act of writing something down can itself become a form of modelling:

> If asked beforehand whether I would use any modelling strategies in developing my subject knowledge, I would have probably answered 'no'. However, in trying to memorise the hierarchy of classification, I found it useful to write things down. It gave me the added visual aspect to support my learning.
>
> (student quote)

Practising operations

Closely related to the process of modelling is that of trying out ideas and applying them in a 'problem-solving' situation. This can enable a deeper and more secure type of learning to take place, because it forces us to apply the knowledge we have learned in one situation to another and extend our 'situated cognition'. Investigations in learning (Vygotsky 1978; Lave 1988) recognise that the activity in which knowledge is developed and deployed is not separable from or ancillary to learning and cognition. In other words, the situation in which knowledge is learned is fundamental to our understanding – we cannot separate what we learn from the way we have learned it. Particularly in mathematics, students can often manipulate algorithms, routines and definitions they have acquired at school, but have little idea how to apply these in another context. Working through examples can develop 'relational understanding' (Skemp 1989) which will endure after the particular context for the learning has been forgotten. As in the case of modelling ideas, this strategy cannot be used on its own, but as a way of reinforcing and clarifying knowledge presented in another way:

> I was able to work through a variety of examples and was surprised at the answers. So I practised operations. Then I tried to think through why the answers were surprising and decided to ask for help (because help was readily available).
>
> (student quote)

> By physically doing the task, I was able to see clearly and would remember which cylinder had the larger capacity.
>
> (student quote)

> I was, to a large degree, rediscovering rather than forming new understandings ... However, I am unsure how effective this format would be for ... developing completely new understandings.
>
> (student quote)

The real power of this tool is manifest in the process of self-assessment, both before the learning process (see 'Auditing' above) and afterwards, in order to reflect upon whether we have developed the knowledge and understanding we require. Particularly if part of a revision aid of worked examples from a textbook, practising operations can give us immediate feedback.

Teaching others – classroom experience

The inclusion of teaching and classroom experience within our toolkit of strategies relates strongly to the principal purpose for which we as teachers are seeking to develop our subject knowledge – in order to teach others.

> My last memories of studying volume and capacity are at secondary school. I have never been sure of the difference between the two. Preparing for the student presentations on measures clarified volume and capacity for me.
>
> (student quote)

> I felt that the best strategy for me was planning to teach the subject, as it made me think not just about what I would teach, but also about how I would teach it.
>
> (student quote)

Learning from classroom experience can involve a variety of related activities. It can be a process of learning alongside the children, in which case we are developing our pedagogic knowledge along with our subject knowledge, and in a form which relates directly to the strategies we will need to employ in order to make that knowledge available to children:

> Children sometimes ask simple but very valid questions which adults can learn from ... This experience showed me that it is possible to learn alongside the children, but it was useful to have some basic knowledge first.
>
> (student quote)

> Teaching children made me aware that I had an 'instrumental' understanding of some maths. I knew that -(-3) is +3. Thinking how to explain this to children developed my knowledge and understanding.
>
> (student quote)

Many teachers would feel insecure in knowing no more than the children in a particular situation; it could be seen as an example of 'the blind leading the blind'. However, if we are prepared to admit that we don't know the answers, and are prepared to find out alongside the children using first-hand enquiry, we are much more likely to develop new or existing knowledge in a form which they can understand. Wilson *et al.* (1987), in investigating beginning secondary teachers' subject-matter knowledge, concluded that, during the course of teaching, existing subject knowledge is transformed as beginning teachers evolve new understanding of subject matter when they begin to teach their subject to children. The transformation of teachers' subject knowledge, coupled with knowledge of the competence of the children, is at the heart of the teaching process, whatever methods are employed. The teacher may act as instructor, demonstrator, guide, catalyst, facilitator, questioner, challenger, organiser, provider ... Whatever the teacher's roles, 'teaching others' is a powerful strategy for learning and developing knowledge so that we hold our understanding in a communicable form.

Other ways of learning in the classroom can involve talking with knowledgeable teachers and other adults, or watching their practice. This can become a form of direct teaching, but again ensures that the knowledge gained is both pedagogic and conceptual.

Summary

In this chapter we have considered some of the factors that influence learning and provided a toolkit of learning strategies. While the learning style may be a fairly fixed characteristic of an individual, 'both nature/nuture in its roots' (Keefe 1987), learning strategies may vary according to the context for learning, the environment and a range of practical considerations. The strategies described above could be categorised in a variety of different ways and are rarely employed exclusively. For example, peer group learning could be considered as a combination of 'collaborative learning' and 'direct teaching', or observing others plan and teach could be viewed as a combination of 'direct teaching' and 'classroom experience'. The purpose for learning can be a powerful motivational force, and it is not surprising that 'classroom experience' seems to be the strategy that is most influential for many students who are aiming to be teachers, not mathematicians or scientists.

The experience of the students at Goldsmiths College who have used many of these strategies has provided evidence of their success, but also indicated potential pitfalls if they are not applied thoughtfully and reflectively. It is vitally important that we evaluate the effectiveness of our learning throughout the process, but especially when we consider ourselves to have 'finished'. Looking back at our initial audit, concept maps or self-administered tests, in what ways have we expanded our range of knowledge, or achieved greater depth of understanding? Are we now fulfilling the requirements of relevant tests, university or national criteria (for example, the standards in DfEE Circular 4/98)? Can we now express the major concepts in language appropriate to the age group we are teaching? What might be the 'key questions' we would want to ask children in order to challenge their understanding? Confident answers to these questions might indicate that we have succeeded in developing our 'knowledge to teach' at a level sufficient for our needs.

References

Department for Education and Employment (DfEE) (1998) *Teaching: High Status, High Standards, Requirements for Courses of Initial Teacher Training, Circular 4/98*, London: DfEE.

Doyle, W. (1978) 'Paradigms for research into teacher effectiveness', in L.S. Shulman (ed.) *Review of Research in Education 5*, Itasca, Illinois: Peacock.

George, D. (1995) *Gifted Education: Identification and Provision*, London: Fulton.

Guetzkow, H., Kelly, E.L. and McKeachie, W.J. (1954) 'An experimental comparison of recitation, discussion and tutorial methods in college teaching', *Journal of Educational Psychology* 45: 193–209.

Keefe, J.W. (1987) *Learning Style – Theory and Practice*, (1904 Association Drive, Reston, Virginia 22091–1598): NASSP.

Lave, J. (1988) *Cognition in Practice*, Boston, Mass.: Cambridge.

Riding, R. and Cheema, I. (1991) 'Cognitive styles – an overview and integration', *Educational Psychology* 11, 3 and 4: 193–215.

Ross, S. and Scanlon, E. (1995) *Open Science: Distance Teaching and Open Learning of Science Subjects*, London: Paul Chapman.

Russell, T., Qualter, A. and McGuigan, L. (1994) *Evaluation of the Implementation of Science in the National Curriculum Key Stages 1, 2 and 3, Vol. 1*, London: School Curriculum and Assessment Authority (SCAA).

Skemp, R. (1989) *Mathematics in the Primary School*, London: Routledge.

Vygotsky, L.S. (1978) *Mind in Society,* Cambridge, Mass.: Harvard University Press.

Wilson, S.M., Shulman, L.S. and Rickert, A.E. (1987) '150 different ways of knowing: representations of knowledge in teaching', in J. Calderhead (ed.) *Exploring Teachers' Thinking*, London: Cassell.

6 From starting point to fair copy

Reading, writing and thinking

Margaret Mallett and Anna Mallett

Introduction

Few things can seem more intimidating than a page with just a title or an idea for a piece of writing. In this chapter, reading and writing are held together as complementary and dynamic processes as the writer journeys from starting point to fair copy. Although writers have different approaches, there are some strategies that will help most students. Both library skills, more diverse now that we have computer searches and CD-ROMs to consult as well as books and journals, and study skills, how to use particular texts for your own purposes, are important and covered throughout this book.

However, writing a good essay, report or longer study is not just a matter of understanding methods of retrieval. It is to do with controlling your material, whether it is from secondary sources alone – in other words drawing on the published findings and analyses of others to create your argument – or introduces the results of first-hand enquiry. In many kinds of educational writing the two kinds of research, library-based and empirical, have to be integrated into a coherent account, and we include a section on how this might be achieved.

Throughout the chapter, reference is made to the experience of ten final year students following a primary BA(Ed.) with English before, during and after completing their 10,000-word English curriculum assignments. At the end of their course, each student filled in a questionnaire about planning and carrying out this partly classroom-based dissertation (see Appendix 6.1). Unless it is intimated that a student comment or observation is from a tutorial or other context, all quoted utterances are taken from the questionnaire. The items are based on feedback to the tutor over some years and include questions about which strategies seemed most helpful at particular stages in the work. It is not suggested that we can generalise from such a small sample; rather, the information from the questionnaire is used illustratively. Nevertheless, taking heed of the 'voices' in the case studies should help minimise the pains and problems and maximise the pleasures and satisfactions of academic writing.

The stages through which we move from blank page to fair copy structure this chapter, beginning with clarifying the task and finding a focus, moving to carrying out classroom-based enquiry, structuring your argument and producing the final work.

Clarifying the task

Whether you are writing a short 3,000-word assignment or a dissertation of 10,000 words or more, you need to keep in mind that academic writing is essentially systematic. Of course, a main purpose is to learn more about your topic, whether it is to do with children's mathematical concepts, planning science investigations or improving literacy. But each writing task should also move you forward in your control over the intellectual skills of analysing material, comparing viewpoints and arguing your case.

This is true whichever institution you attend and whatever your topic. But there may be some other requirements for a particular task at a particular college, and you need to read the course documentation on scope, presentation and referencing at an early stage. Let us make the point by describing two very different assignments at the institution of one of the authors – Goldsmiths College. Our second year students are asked (for their shorter 'English in Education' assignment) to write up how they carried out a miscue analysis (a diagnostic reading assessment), and to present their results in the form of a diagram. They are also required to provide a short analysis of what they have learnt from the test results about the child's reading competence, and to suggest strategies to support progress. The assignment instructions, reinforced by the discipline of keeping to a 1,000-word maximum, make this necessarily a focused writing task. Students do not, for example, have space for the luxury of a detailed account of different viewpoints on assessment. This task requires the writer to judge what is essential and what can reasonably be left out. It calls for both an ability to focus on the detail of the child's performance in certain given categories *and* some of the same skills of condensation required in good summary writing in the concluding comments. Different intellectual abilities are called for in another 'English in Education' assignment, in which students are asked to write an account entitled 'Making a book with a child'. This involves a careful account of a series of one-to-one sessions and an assessment of the strategies employed by the student teacher to support progress. In this sense it sounds similar to the first task described. However, as the advice for this 3,000-word assignment makes clear, this example needs to be placed within a wider context of current understandings about how literacy develops and the teacher's role in that development. Here is a brief extract from Rochelle's assignment which indicates how she has wider issues in mind – in this case the challenge non-narrative kinds of writing can pose for everyone – while analysing one child's progress. E has reached Year 6 without breaking through to fluent reading and writing, although his intelligence is evident from his control over spoken language. He has decided to make a book of unusual inventions illustrated by careful and entertaining diagrams.

> During the project E learnt a great deal about non-fiction; elements of the genre were drawn on in making his book. To begin with, we looked at David Macaulay's *How Things Work* which gave E an understanding of important aspects of the genre. We looked at the diagrams and noted their detail and use of labelling to describe certain parts of the illustration. We also noted the use of captions and the grammatical structure they followed. I was concerned that E might find difficulty in handling this formal writing structure as a struggling reader and writer. As Valerie Cherrington writes, 'These structures do not form part of our oral culture' (Cherrington 1990: 159).

This integration of principles and practice demands profound reflection both on the particular classroom example and on the related theoretical issues explored in relevant reading. Rochelle's 'voice' is that of a reflective practitioner using her reading to illuminate her practice. The skills and abilities called for in each of the tasks described here are valuable, but success depends on understanding which set of criteria you are trying to meet. In other words – read carefully the relevant section in your course booklet!

The students whose questionnaire responses inform this chapter were required to carry out an action inquiry (evaluating their own practice) or case study (assessing one school's approach to an aspect of English or one teacher's strategies). This involved them in acquiring research skills of systematic observation, careful data collection and analysis. Further, the required selective review of the literature needed to relate strongly to the issues in the classroom work.

There are other kinds of worthwhile research, including library-based philosophical studies on a range of topics including assessment, particular areas and aspects of the curriculum, and evaluation of official documentation. The latter kind of writing calls for careful analysis of ideas and issues and their implications, as well as the ability to synthesise the fruits of the work of a number of scholars. While different viewpoints are evaluated, the writer's own argument and its justification is a crucial element of the work. It would be unfortunate if this kind of study was discouraged as a consequence of a more classroom-based approach to teacher education, however valuable empirical studies may be. In the assignment which is the main example in this chapter, some effort to maintain the rigour often associated with library studies is made by giving weight to the review of the literature which usually precedes and contextualises the classroom work.

Whichever kind of study you are required to produce, it will mean systematic effort. One obvious way to make things easier is to record your references in the required format from the start of your work and remember to put in the page numbers for quotations you may decide to use. Tutors usually keep copies of successful past assignments for current students to consult. The content and structure of some assignments is prescribed: for example, a mathematics assignment might require a student to write up plans and evaluations of a series of lessons on measurement. Where there is more choice, as in the case of the students writing the 10,000-word English dissertations referred to in the present study, it is helpful if students are given some idea of the sort of topics past students have selected.

Once a broad area is chosen – for example 'early years non-fiction reading and writing', 'drama and writing' or 'computers in English' (all areas chosen by the students in this study) – the task now is to read round the topic and to narrow the focus.

Finding a focus

At this stage you need to carry out some preliminary library research. Check through reading lists and note which texts are essential and which optional. Tutors often star key texts in course booklists for particular topics. Guidance on recent official reports and research in journals, as well as key books, is also given in lectures, seminars and tutorials. Once you track down a couple of recommended texts their bibliographies will draw your attention to others. There are now a great many aids to finding the information you need and university librarians will nearly always give some help with using CD-ROM, microfiche and the internet. But at the preliminary focus-seeking stage you can use the library computer to track down the key texts. Particularly if your study is over 5,000 words, you need also at some stage to carry out a computer search of your subject to check you are aware of any relevant major research study. You need to be imaginative, as the same phenomenon can be differently named. For my non-fiction search I looked under the following: information retrieval, children's information books, EXEL project, non-narrative reading/writing, functional literacy.

As you read in the general area, two things can usefully be kept in mind:

- Is there an aspect of the large topic that appeals to you?
- Are there some questions that occur to you, perhaps arising from teaching practice and school visits?

Asked about this stage of her work, L said that on her last teaching practice she found one of the greatest challenges was to make writing tasks useful and enjoyable for children at the beginning of Key Stage 1. As she browsed through the literature she found that some teachers use role play and drama as a way of energising children's writing. A proposition began to take shape – how far can exploring a text through drama lead to range and quality in children's writing? L found herself reading in different ways for different purposes. What is known as 'skimming', the very swift reading of a text to get the gist of information or argument, can be necessary. L found the contents pages, chapter and section headings and sometimes the index were all helpful here. 'Scanning' – where a particular date or name is sought – was helpful to L in finding quickly whether a book or journal mentioned key research studies or names of scholars interested in writing and drama. Reading moves into a different gear when we make a close evaluation of an argument or research study. For me, one of the most inspirational accounts of this highly active and reflective sort of reading is in Lunzer and Gardner's book *The Effective Use of Reading* (Lunzer and Gardner 1979). This critical reading informs the literature review necessary in dissertations, and sometimes in a shorter form, essays. It also helps us make the connection between relevant work and thinking in our area and the more modest and focused question we decide to address.

The notes made during this preliminary research need to be strong and useful. One student known to me underlines his notes in different colours to indicate their status – red for major points, yellow for sub-points and blue for useful examples supporting the main point. Another student peppers her notes with asides like 'Does this contradict what X says in his book?' and 'Remember to include this in my Ch. 2 perhaps?' Develop personalised shorthand codes to speed up the work. Have a small box file or a loose-leaf file with you, and be meticulous over references. Get them down in a form you can quickly transfer to your word-processor as the bibliography starts to take shape. Do not spend too long reading round the topic. P felt she had lingered too long in the library before making a choice and producing a global plan to show her tutor.

While a detailed plan like that shown in Box 6.1 is best left until after you have agreed a structure with your tutor, you need at this stage a working title and some provisional research questions. Writing often has a heuristic function, and even brief notes on what you plan to do can help you find out what you really want to investigate and develop your thinking. When it comes to very short essays, some people find the argument develops its own momentum and a plan in the head is all that is needed. Others always need the security of a written plan. Where you will be having a tutorial, something written down to provide a focus for your discussion is essential.

This chapter is mainly concerned with the planning and structuring of course work and dissertations. However, answers written under examination conditions

Box 6.1 Planning the dissertation

Working title/area

Main research question and supplementary questions

Global structure

Abstract

Give brief information about the topic and scope of the work (e.g. 'This study examines ... After a selective review of the literature there is an analysis of the work of class/group of children aged ... which concentrates particularly on questions to do with ... A careful review of the findings seems in line with ... and the writer argues that ...'). For examples of abstracts see the UKRA *Reading* journal, which includes articles detailing the classroom work of practising teachers.

Introduction

This is more detailed than the abstract and should be an invitation to the work. Why is the area under study important? What are some of the issues? What are the main aims/focus of the study? There is no blueprint, but students often include an anecdote close to the central issues of the study or some reasons for choosing the topic. It is important to sound enthusiastic.

A brief invitation to each chapter and its function in the whole study is usually included (e.g. 'Chapter 1 presents a selective review of the literature which includes a careful consideration of ——'s recent research which relates strongly to my own area of interest ... There is a justification for the design of the study and the methods of data collection in Chapter 2.').

Chapter 1

This is nearly always a selective review of the literature. Subheadings help organise your work – but do not have too many as it risks disturbing the flow of your argument.

Chapter 2 The design of the study

- Remind the reader of your research questions.
- Mention the kind of research – action research or case study – and justify methods of data collection.
- Set out details of community, school, class and children and aims and plan of empirical work.

Chapter 3 The story of the work

If you have carried out a series of lessons or observations, a chronological organisation of what happened is fine, but we also need reasons for what you did and explanations for what happened. If your research has taken the form of a case study of one school's approach to, for example, 'special needs' or 'information communications technology', your 'story' may best be told without being tied to a time sequence organisation. You may wish to refer to interviews, questionnaire responses and observation more flexibly.

Chapter 4 Analysis of findings

One good way of structuring this is under your research questions used as subheadings.

Conclusion

This should not just repeat what is in the final chapter. There will be some overlap, but the conclusion will be less detailed and does not normally include subheadings or quotations from secondary sources. It can be quite short, but needs to make clear what the main findings are. While you should not make great claims for a modest piece of work perhaps based on one example, you should write a strong account of how you think your work has illuminated the issues under consideration. If you write best within a clear framework you might decide to organise your conclusion round three or four main points, making this structure explicit at the beginning. (e.g. 'This conclusion assesses three main aspects of the study: the most dramatic findings and how they may affect my future practice; an element of the work that surprised me; the degree to which my data collection methods were useful').

Bibliography

Lists of children's books and resources mentioned

Appendix

also need a clear focus and some advice about this is set out in the section 'A note on different kinds of writing task' and in Vignette 6.3 (pp. 107–10).

Talking about progress with tutors or peers

The constructivist model, which provides a theoretical underpinning to all the chapters in this book, presents an essentially active learner. Spoken language is a powerful tool in organising our thinking, particularly when we are wrestling with new information and ideas. The response of others to our expressed notions stimulates us to clarify and if necessary modify them. A short tutorial, even if in times of increasing financial restraint it is with two or three other students rather than one-to-one with a tutor, can be most helpful even when the assignment is a short one. Students following the Goldsmiths BA(Ed.) mostly appreciated the small group tutorials to help them get their ideas into a clear structure in their 3,000-word language essay. The comments and questions of other students help to clarify their own ideas and provide welcome interest and stimulation. For a longer essay or dissertation such help is even more important. Yet, as tutors know, some students do not take advantage of this support, and while some students manage well enough without, the finished writing of others indicates they could have benefited from guidance.

All ten of the undergraduates who were the subjects referred to in this study ticked the 'talking with a tutor' choice in Question 2 of the questionnaire as being either the most helpful or second most helpful way of identifying a focus once the main topic of the long essay was chosen. Where 'talking with a tutor' was placed second, students selected either option (d), research in the library, or (e), discussing the possibilities with the class teacher, as the most important factor. Now that parts of the primary curriculum are fairly prescribed, for example the National Literacy Strategy objectives and the daily numeracy session, negotiation with the class teacher might assume greater importance in deciding on a focus. All the students took advantage of the half-hour tutorial provided after their preliminary reading and reflecting on a draft plan was complete, and all but one took advantage of the second tutorial which included an offer on the tutor's part to skim through first drafts of chapters either before or during the tutorial. What, then, did they consider the tutorials achieved?

First, the earlier tutorial helped achieve a coherent global structure for the work. The sooner a clear structure is achieved, the easier it is to read productively for each section or chapter. As E pointed out, however, the tutor's expertise can only be used if students have prepared for their tutorial, producing a draft global plan and some specific questions and issues. P remarked on the tutor's role in 'sharpening up the plan of the study' and making sure there was a clear, manageable structure and at least the promise of a coherent argument. The other major task of the first tutorial is to discuss the classroom-based work and make sure the design and scope is appropriate. It is extremely important that the planned work will be of benefit to the children involved as well as to the student researcher. In social science research in general, universities are concerned that certain ethical principles be heeded by tutors and students. No procedure must risk physical or psychological harm to subjects. Potentially disturbing questions should not be asked; in the work of the student group mentioned, questionnaires and structured interview questions were shown to tutor and class teacher before students went ahead. Where procedures are not part of normal everyday practice, the consent of parents may have to be sought; tutors and class teachers will give guidance here. 'Everyday practice' includes class, group and individual work in lesson time which has been approved by the class teacher. Interviews and questionnaires during breaks and lunchtimes are of a different status. If in doubt – seek advice. Usually, however, the input of student teachers is welcomed by both teachers and pupils.

Some of the students sought reassurance at their first tutorial that their project was sufficiently scholarly. While welcoming the challenge of a sustained piece of work, they wanted to make sure it represented the best that they could do, since it would carry a lot of marks. Although the students had carried out and evaluated lessons and children's activities in several areas of their course, for most of them this was the first systematic action research they had attempted. Action research can consist of a series of lessons which are planned, carried out and evaluated more systematically and in greater depth than usual in order to inform future practice. Data such as children's writing and transcripts of lessons are carefully collected and analysed, and the views of other professionals, usually the tutor or class teacher, are sought at particular points in the work, a procedure known as triangulation. M writes: 'It is in the spirit of Vygotsky's advice that you can learn from someone more expert and mature.' In case either writer of this article or any other college tutor becomes too flattered about our role in helping students do well, another student remarked, 'In the end you have to get down to it yourself.'

Someone else was heard on leaving a tutorial to mutter, 'I came out of there more confused than when I went in.'

After the first tutorial, students filled in the outline shown in Figure 6.1. There are alternatives to this suggested structure where reference to literature is more integrated with the argument and design of the study. In any case, any model is best seen as a flexible framework which can be modified to suit a student's purposes. Perusal of the plan at this stage enables the tutor to look through the crucial global structure of the work and to add any comments, book suggestions and so on before returning it. A well-structured plan, with the key ideas organised and positioned, can mean the assignment can be written straight from it. Far from being a straitjacket, the plan can be a guiding framework that allows the writer to control the analysis and let their own 'voice' come through. I have found that once students have written drafts of both the review of the literature and their account of the 'story' of their work, they are sometimes sufficiently in control of the material to integrate the two elements in the work more closely. For example, L brought the fruits of some of her analysis of Graves' notion of 'conferencing' – discussion with a child of their plans for writing – to the assessment of her lessons. Links like this made a study integrated and powerful. Some students find that once the global plan is agreed, a more detailed plan for each chapter arranged under subheadings helps. You may decide not to keep all the subheadings in the final draft – too many can disturb the flow of the account – but they ensure all relevant elements are included.

While it is not necessary, even if time allowed, for a tutor to read every word of the first draft of a long essay, most of the ten students found it helpful at the second tutorial for the tutor to look through some of the work.

Carrying out classroom-based work

Many education assignments at undergraduate and post-graduate level require students to carry out an empirical study in school. The research question is the key factor in designing a classroom-based study. In the section of this chapter called 'Finding a focus', the steps towards refining the question at the heart of the study were briefly indicated. Most students begin with a broad area. K, for example, wanted to investigate an aspect of children's understanding of written genres. A narrower focus needed to be arrived at before the classroom work could be designed. After discussion with her tutor and class teacher, K planned to carry out an action research inquiry based on her own work with a group of Year 4 children talking about a traditional and a modern version of Cinderella. Her question became: 'How far can class talk about fairy tales secure children's understanding of the main features of the genre?' Although this was not an issue when K carried out her study, students may find English studies have to take account of the objectives of the National Literacy Strategy's Literacy Hour. Requirements mean that the time of teachers and children can be used less flexibly, and this affects how classroom projects are carried out.

The ten BA (Ed.) students mentioned in this chapter were required to carry out an action research enquiry (see Bell 1987). This fits well with the cycle of teaching – planning, carrying out teaching, and assessment – as successful practice can feed into the next cycle of planning. This kind of research also has the advantage of not requiring children to be removed from their regular lessons. Action research has been criticised for being subjective and too much like the kind of evaluation teachers do anyway as part of good practice. However, it can be as systematic as other kinds of research if the methods of data collection are carefully designed and carried out. You need to set out the strengths and possible limitations of any technique you use – interview, questionnaire, note-taking, observing, videoing, collecting samples of writing and tape-recording – and how you consider it will illuminate your research question (see also Chapter 9).

As you will know from your school visits and teaching practice, classrooms are lively, and sometimes creatively chaotic places where the unexpected is likely to occur. No two days are the same. Research, on the other hand, needs to be orderly and approached calmly. You need to have your aims and plans carefully in your mind and, preferably, also in your research notebook.

If time allows, it is very helpful to observe activities in the classroom in which you will be carrying out your work. P visited children in the nursery on several occasions just to observe how young children approach computers and how the nursery team support them. This helped her refine her research questions.

Once the research begins there are a number of ways of making it disciplined. If you are taking a series of lessons in which you will be trying out some particular strategy, it is helpful to make it clear that the work will last for five 2-hour sessions on consecutive afternoons. Keep the data collected in each session separate so that you can note progression in the work. Ask the class teacher or another teacher or student teacher to assess your work by showing them children's writing or transcripts of their response in lessons. If you set out some questions you can then carry out a structured interview (an interview where key questions are prepared in written form but where the interviewer has some flexibility over the order of questions, the precise way in which they are phrased and the time spent on each) and include it in your study as evidence of triangulation. Triangulation may involve the seeking out of another professional person's opinion on work carried out by another researcher. A classroom teacher who knows the children well is in a good position to give an informed view about the success of a series of lessons, providing the triangulation which will increase the confidence of the student researcher in the usefulness of their findings. It is helpful to write down some questions to structure your triangulation interview.

For example K, whose work on traditional tales is mentioned above, showed the class teacher the transcripts of the children's discussion on the chosen fairy tale; she asked how far the teacher agreed there were signs of growing understanding of features of the fairy-tale genre, including the role of magic, the importance of numbers (three wishes, twelve princesses, and so on) and the use of a special kind of book language. It is best not to make the interview too long or too involved, given the time restraints on researcher and teacher.

If you are working with the whole class you might like to concentrate your analysis mainly on the response of perhaps six children, two able, two of average ability in the class and two who find their work difficult. At master's level, particularly if your study is over 20,000 words, you may need to consider the response of all the children. In a shorter assignment, or one at undergraduate level, the scope can be more modest. You can prepare short case studies of the selected group of children, including perhaps their reading age, interests, strengths and possible areas where they need support. Two major kinds of data useful in school-based action research are children's writing examples and tape-recordings of lessons and interviews. Where writing is included, background information about age, gender and the ability of the child, date when the work was done, the context of the writing (was it a response to a story, an outing, etc.?) is nearly always the minimum necessary. Depending on the purpose, you may also need to indicate National Curriculum levels. (The Centre for Language in Primary Education has some writing scales which teachers are finding a useful complement to the National Curriculum levels. See *Language Matters*, 1995/6: 3–8.) Tape-recordings also have to be dated and contextualised. You need to ask the class teacher for permission and to explain to the children why you need to record their discussion. Tape-recording is a useful way of recording precise detail of utterances. Try to transcribe your tape-recordings soon after each session. The authors of this chapter know from experience what a terrifying task it is to do this at the end of five or six sessions which all seem to merge into one when you try to remember the texture of each occasion. Remember, too, that your research notebook is one of the most helpful tools. Jottings here can include snippets of conversation, social behaviour and gestures accompanying children's comments. This will help you recapture the lesson. Include the tape-recording transcripts in an appendix and quote sections from them to support the main findings of your study.

Make sure the children benefit from your input, and try to offer something to the school in recognition of their kindness in allowing you to carry out your work. One of us was carrying out research into non-fiction for a doctorate and in return for the school's co-operation gave some support to two young learners with reading difficulties and a short talk to staff and parents about choosing non-fiction books. Always write to the class teacher and the head teacher to thank them for their help when your work is completed.

One last thing you need to bear in mind is that those of us who go into school are sometimes given privileged access to information which should be kept confidential. Children's confidentiality should be guarded by using pseudonyms, or in some cases the first letter of the first name. Check with the school before including sensitive or confidential information in case studies.

Writing up the fair draft (including referencing)

Integrating primary and secondary evidence

Primary evidence is any unpublished finding and is likely to mean all the data – tape-recordings, observation notes and children's writing – that a student has collected during their study. Secondary evidence is found in the published writings of other scholars and must be carefully acknowledged. Your research focus comes from the selective review of the literature. When the results of the findings in the classroom are discussed, you need to make some links between your own modest results and the findings of other scholars mentioned. You might, for instance, want to write something like: 'This is a small-scale study and results cannot be generalised. However, the findings do seem consistent with the work of . . .'. This then links you with a community of scholars.

Integrating the reading of print with diagrams and visual aids

The way in which both school children and students at university integrate their reading of print with visual aids is a relatively under-researched area. In education books and research papers, diagrams are used to give the results of surveys, examination results, models of learning – there are also annotated samples of records of children's progress in an area of the curriculum, perhaps pictures of children's activities, especially in professional journals and magazines and books and articles which lean towards the professional rather than the academic.

A recent and useful study on learning from text and visual aids at different stages was carried out in Australia (Moore and Scevak 1997). They looked at how readers of different ages focused on three levels of outcome: details, main ideas and more complex inferential level of themes. The research approach was most interesting – subjects were asked to 'think aloud' as they grappled with the reading and the visual aids. While students' strategies in coping with history texts and their related visual aids remained similar from 11–14 years, the older students showed more flexible approaches to scientific kinds of writing and the associated visual aids. The researchers concluded that the chronological organisation of history writing was a more sympathetic form, particularly for younger students, than the non-narrative organisation of science texts. It was also suggested that direct teaching of reading strategies, not least in integrating reading of text and visual aid, might be appropriate and useful in science.

There is evidence that learners who use a wide range of strategies in a purposeful way gain a firmer grip on the material (see, for example, Wade *et al.* 1990). Charts and diagrams will make your work more visually interesting and can be used to summarise your results. If, for example, you were looking at boys' and girls' interventions during a class reading of a novel, you might make a table to show the relative number of utterances in one or more contexts. Look in books and journals to see how other researchers have used visual aids. You may base your own charts and diagrams on these, but need to put something like: 'Based on the table in Czerniewska (1992: 141)'.

Photographs can be most helpful in communicating the flavour of a lesson or to show the quality of a display. They should not be stuck in just for the sake of it, however. They must be referred to in the body of the text if they are placed in the appendix.

Writing well, clear expression, grammar and punctuation

As you assemble your first draft, you need initially to get a grip on what seems to have emerged. When you feel in control of the materials, both primary and secondary, you can begin to assemble your argument. You cannot include everything. Think of the reader and what they need to be told to understand your findings. It is not a matter of sticking in any interesting but random bit of information. Academic writing is to do with analysis – not just what happened but why it happened and what its likely significance is. The organisation of your findings and the power of your argument and the sense of your 'voice' expressing it are crucial. However, to communicate effectively in the academic register, you have to follow certain conventions. Your thoughts need to be expressed grammatically and your writing conventionally punctuated and well spelt. Flexibility and appropriateness of vocabulary are also important.

Grammar

Grammar or syntax refers to the rules governing the construction of sentences. A study of language, its structures and functions, can be interesting in its own right. It is also true that we might reasonably expect an educated person to know and understand the main terminology as a matter of general knowledge. But does a knowledge of the structure of language, of sentence forms, tense, person, parts of speech and so on, help the writer? The implication in the 1995 National

Curriculum English programmes, which feature a standard English and language study strand at each age phase, is that it does. The *Framework for Teaching* (DfEE 1998), which was distributed to schools in March 1998 to inform the planning and content of the literacy hour beginning in September 1998, goes even further in prescribing the teaching of grammar. Thus a culture which takes this approach to English lessons and the teaching of literacy is being put in place, and it remains to be seen how far children's literacy improves.

In my experience, students whose written expression is not clear are more likely to have a difficulty over clear thinking about their topic and full control of the material. Awareness of the needs of the reader is also important – as the student whose difficulties are described in Vignette 6.1 discovered. Nevertheless, I find it helpful to have to hand a reference book like McArthur's (1992) *The Oxford Companion to the English Language* when writing. It is alphabetically organised and interesting to browse through. An alternative is David Crystal's (1987) *The Cambridge Encyclopaedia of Language*. The other thing to point out here is the important role of punctuation in highlighting the grammatical import of sentences, phrases and words – more about this below.

Vignette 6.1 Dissertation – the case of the never-ending sentences

Problem

P spoke in an articulate manner about her study. Once she began to write, however, she produced long sentences with embedded clauses.

Solution

P was advised to imagine a reader struggling with long sentences where meaning became difficult to gain quickly. She looked at strategies to break up the longer sentences by having two or more shorter ones or by using semi-colons and colons (see Figure 6.2). As a result, her writing gained a new clarity and energy, and the final draft achieved a high grade.

Punctuation

Punctuation helps us compensate in writing for what we can achieve through pause, pace and expression in speech. The conventional marks serve a grammatical role; commas, for example, separate words and phrases. Language is dynamic and usage changes, however irritated this makes those who believe there is a universal and enduring standard of correctness from which none of us should deviate. The general trend is towards having fewer punctuation markings and changed usage – for example the dash is tending to take over where once a phrase was separated by commas. The following definition gives welcome emphasis to the main purpose of punctuation, which is to clarify meaning. 'The practice in writing or print of using a set of marks to regulate texts and clarify their meanings, principally by separating or linking words, phrases, and clauses and by indicating parenthesis and asides' (McArthur 1992: 824).

Students vary considerably in their control over the finer points of punctuation. Those wishing to reflect on issues in learning to punctuate would find *Learning about Punctuation* useful and readable (Hall and Robinson 1996). It includes interesting accounts of research on child and adult learners of punctuation. My only quibble is that it does not include an index.

Although the conventions of punctuation evolved over the years in a partly arbitrary way, neither employers nor examiners are tolerant of unconventional usage. Those wishing to become more secure over the use of colons, semi-colons and dashes will often find guidance in introductions to dictionaries, as well as under specific entries, for example *The Collins School Dictionary* (Hanks 1989). The main conventions are also well covered in *The Oxford Companion to the English Language* (McArthur 1992) and in *English for Primary Teachers* (Wray and Medwell 1997). Box 6.2 draws on all of these in providing a quick checklist of some of the main punctuation conventions students ask about. We must remember that use of punctuation is to some extent a matter of personal choice. We might choose to have two short sentences rather than use a semi-colon, and we may separate a phrase using commas, brackets or dashes.

Spelling and vocabulary

Computer spell checks and dictionaries on CD-ROMs help those who feel insecure about their spelling (although difficulties may not be discovered until examination conditions prevail). However, such innovations have not replaced dictionaries in book form. For a good all-purpose dictionary, you might consider buying or using in the library *Collins School Dictionary* (Hanks 1989) which has 180,000 in entries in the current edition. All the words qualify for a fresh paragraph, which makes it user-friendly.

Most of us have favourite words and phrases and need to seek synonyms to avoid over-use of the same vocabulary. Your computer may provide you with a thesaurus or you can use one of the print ones in the library.

Box 6.2 Punctuation points students often query

Ways of separating a phrase	*Many children find computers make writing easier, and more interesting, than writing by hand.* *Many children find computers make writing easier (and more interesting) than writing by hand.* *Many children find computers make writing easier – and more interesting – than writing by hand.*
Semi-colon	This is often used instead of two short sentences or a conjunction to link two parallel statements. *Children enjoy outdoor play. It restores their enthusiasm.* *Children enjoy outdoor play; it restores their enthusiasm.* It is used also to link two **independent clauses*** within a **compound sentence****, when a **conjunctive adverb***** connects them. *The teacher remarked that she had never organised a school fete; however, she added that she had always taught in schools in which the parents were keen to organise events.* *an **independent clause** is a clause which is sentence-like in its construction, with elements like a subject and an object. **a **compound sentence** has two or more main clauses. ***a **conjunctive adverb** has a connective role, as 'however' has in the example.

Colon	A colon is often placed before a summary, a quotation or, as in the example, a list. *Angela dropped her school-bag and the contents fell on the floor: pencils, pens, calculator, ruler and some poetry books.* It can also introduce a following statement. *Take it or leave it: the choice is yours.*
Apostrophes	Apostrophes show where one or more letters have been missed out. *It's* is a contraction of *it is.* In *'The cat licked its kittens'*, its is possessive and needs no apostrophe. The possessive form of plural nouns ending in *s* is usually made by adding an apostrophe after the *s.* Other plural nouns need *'s.* *Teachers' books.* *Children's desks.*

Referencing, appendix material and keys

It was suggested earlier that a system for meticulous recording of references and page numbers should be put in place at the beginning of the work. This saves time and worry later on when the deadline looms nearer.

The Harvard system

The most widely chosen and recommended reference style is called the Harvard system. In the text, only the author's surname, year of publication and, if required, page number are used. This allows the reading to flow. Full details of all references are given at the end of a text in an alphabetically organised list or bibliography. Details and punctuation can differ according to the house style of a publisher or country of publication. However, in your own writing it is important to chose a style, taking into consideration your institution's recommendations, and then use it systematically. The format given in the sections below has been adapted from Routledge's 'Instructions for Authors' (1998), Bell (1993), and Goldsmiths Educational Studies course documentation.

Some wordprocessing packages, such as Microsoft Word, allow the automatic inclusion of numbered footnotes, but often a bibliographic system is preferred. Reference lists only detail those cited in the text. A bibliography can also include sources used in preparation but not directly cited in the text. It is worth finding out about the expectations of your tutor or supervisor in advance. There are computer programs – specialised databases – available, such as EndNote, which allow automatic creation of bibliographies.

References in the text

The standard format is given below.

Author(s) surname, year of publication:

(Bell 1993)

Page number(s) are added for more specific references or quotes:

(Bell 1993: 26)

Passages are denoted by the start and finish page numbers:

(Bell 1993: 26–28)

You can abbreviate the second number:

(Bell 1993: 115–64)

Variations – some styles use p. for page and pp. for pages. It is also possible to use the abbreviation chap. for chapter:

(Bell 1993, p. 26)

(Bell 1993, pp. 26–28)

(Bell 1993, chap. 3)

For government reports or similar, use the name of the government department or organisation if there is no obvious author:

(DfEE 1998)

Where two authors with the same name are cited separately, initials can be added to distinguish between them:

(Bell, J. 1993: 26)

When there are two authors, both surnames are used:

(Lunzer and Gardner 1979)

Where there are two or more additional authors the first name plus *et al.* is used:

(Wade *et al.* 1990)

Where you are quoting from two or more different sources by the same author published in the same year, a, b, c, etc., are added to denote the chronological sequence:

(Stenhouse 1971a)

(Stenhouse 1971b)

If you quote again from the same source without any intervening references you can use (ibid.) from the Latin *ibidem* – in the same book, chapter or passage. This should never be carried from one chapter to another:

(ibid.) – referring to Stenhouse (1971b), the last reference made

If you quote again from the same source after intervening references, you can use (op. cit.) from the Latin *opere citato* – in the work already quoted. This should be used with the author's name and, if needed, page numbers. It should never be carried from one chapter to another:

in Bell (op. cit.: 27)

Reference lists and bibliographies

The standard format is as follows:

Author(s) surname and initials
If edited – (ed.) or (eds)
Date of publication
Title (underlined in typescript, italic in print – main words have capitals)
Edition (if applicable)
Place of publication: Publisher

Examples

Bell, J. (1993) *Doing Your Research Project*, second edition, Buckingham: Open University Press.

DfEE (1998) *Circular number 4/98 Requirements for Courses of Initial Teacher Training*, London: DfEE.

Lunzer, E. and Gardner, K. (1979) *The Effective Use of Reading*, London: Heinemann.

With papers in journals, the title of the paper is identified with single quotation marks in Britain, double quotation marks in America. The title of the journal is in italics. The volume number and page numbers are included at the end:

Morley, L. (1998) 'All you need is love: feminist pedagogy for empowerment and emotional labour in the academy', *International Journal of Inclusive Education* 2, 1: 15–27.

Wade, S.E., Trathen, W. and Schraw, G. (1990) 'An analysis of spontaneous study strategies', *Reading Research Quarterly* 25: 147–166.

For references to chapters within edited collections, the chapter title is identified by single quotation marks. The title of the book is in italics:

Kelly, A.V. (1980) 'Ideological constraints on curriculum planning', in A.V. Kelly (ed.) *Curriculum Context*, London: Harper and Row.

References by the same author are listed chronologically:

> Stenhouse, L. (1971a) 'The Humanities Curriculum Project: the rationale', *Theory into Practice* 10: 154–62.
>
> Stenhouse, L. (1971b) 'Pupils into students', *Dialogue (Schools Council Newsletter)* 5: 10–12.

In some styles the repeated name is replaced by a line:

> ——(1971b) 'Pupils into students', *Dialogue (Schools Council Newsletter)* 5: 10–12.

For a not yet published book you can substitute (forthcoming) for the date.

For an unpublished source you can identify its status and location after the title – e.g. unpublished MPhil thesis, University of London.

Electronic references should be included detailing what medium it is available through (HTTP, e-mail, etc.) and the address (URL) with access date in brackets:

> DfEE (1998) *Circular number 4/98 Requirements for Courses of Initial Teacher Training*, London. Online. Available HTTP: http://www.open.gov.u/dfee/dfeehome.htm (1 March 1999).

Students often ask about the best way in which to use quotations. Sometimes if the quotation is long you can paraphrase part of it, only quoting the very best line or two. A short phrase can be included as part of a sentence without indenting. E wrote:

> What Wray and Lewis call 'genre exchange' refers to the strategy of asking children to read one kind of writing and write the information in another format: for example children might read about Tudor food and then write menus for a Tudor banquet (Wray and Lewis 1996).

Remember that too many quotations can disturb the flow of your writing. Where quotations add support to your argument, make them serve your purpose and integrate them into your analysis. This is how L skilfully brings another researcher's insight to bear on her own findings:

> Many children were eager to include postscripts to their letters, and this supports Pam Czerniewska's point about children's ability 'to actively work out how the writing system is organised' (Czerniewska 1992: 60).

Appendix material can add to the worth and interest of the study and does not usually contribute to the wordage. Each appendix item should be justifiable and should be referred to in the account. Appendix number and title of the item is necessary and should appear on the contents page of the study. Examples of children's writing and drawing should be well presented and annotated. These points may seem obvious, but a minority of students each year include a large amount of uncontextualised appendix material assuming that the reader will know its relevance, and occasionally candidates do not do children's work the courtesy of neat presentation and labelling. Transcripts of lessons and structured interviews are often included in education studies. It is helpful to include a key explaining basic symbols, as shown in Box 6.3.

Box 6.3 A student's simple key to transcript symbols

CAPITAL LETTERS	Where a word or phrase is spoken loudly
. . .	Signifies a pause
^^^^^^^^	Indicates that utterances overlap

Gordon Wells numbers the utterances in his transcripts so that they can more easily be referred to in the text (see, for example, Wells 1986: 30). Some writers have a column for comments alongside the utterances (see, for example, Mallett 1992: 152–3). This makes it possible to indicate paralinguistic or non-verbal aspects of communication, including aspects of body language like facial expression and gesture, and tone of voice.

It is now a general requirement that essays and dissertations are wordprocessed, and the spell check has greatly helped candidates with secretarial accuracy. However, this does not help with punctuation nor, more fundamentally, with clear and grammatical expression of ideas. Students need also to check that no errors have crept in during printing out – lines missed out and so on.

Tutors are unlikely to be prepared to correct the English and punctuation in drafts of a study or essay, but errors here will reduce the scholarly nature of the work and could affect the grade. As well as carefully proofreading themselves, some candidates ask a friend to go through the draft before the final copy is printed.

A note on different kinds of writing task

Although hopefully much of the advice here applies to writing tasks generally, each kind of assignment represents a particular challenge. The undergraduate long essay or dissertation has been well covered in this chapter and I now turn to writing MA dissertations, short essays and examination answers.

MA dissertations

Like undergraduate studies, MA dissertations can take a number of forms from library-based philosophical approaches to those which gain their main focus from school-based inquiry. Work at master's level is usually longer and we would expect it to move up a gear in the level of analysis achieved. Where there is a classroom-based element, an experienced teacher brings the fruits of their years in school to the study in a way the student teacher is not yet able to do.

Teachers carry out a great deal of professional writing, including reports, assessments, development plans and policies. Not surprisingly, some teachers find returning to academic writing needs some adjustment of approach and may find some of the advice given for undergraduate studies useful.

Short essays

The students who filled in the questionnaire all thought the longer essay made considerably more demands on them – it was a matter not only of length but of achieving a deeper level of analysis. However, short assignments – 3,000 words or under – impose particular kinds of discipline – not least, of course, what several students called 'the brevity discipline'. Each sentence needs to drive the argument on and all the essential points need to be included with just the right amount of detail, as we saw in 'Writing well'. Addressing a given title for an essay is also important, as illustrated in Vignette 6.2. The sections in this chapter on planning and referencing are relevant to shorter essays. They need to be scholarly and to give the impression of a mind at work on an issue.

Vignette 6.2 Essay with given title – not answering the question

Problem

Student X gave endless background on the topic but never addressed herself to the precise question asked. Nothing she wrote was wrong and some of it was quite interesting. She was disappointed with her low grades.

Solution

The problem here was mainly to do with structure. The essays were too much like a series of notes. X needed help in planning a structure for the essay and in developing an argument. After a first burst of reading, she needed to make a plan indicating some different viewpoints and then setting out the case for the one preferred. The second burst of reading needed to identify which scholars supported which approach, so that their names and brief quotations from their work could strengthen her analysis. Examination of relevant research would help provide the examples to support her view and to place these examples at the most appropriate part of the essay.

Writing under examination conditions

This is a special sort of 'first draft' writing and some students feel the lack of the security of a computer spell check and thesaurus. Success depends on planning ahead. You cannot study everything in the same detail, so choose a few areas to look at in depth. Write a key area on a sheet of A4 paper and make some subheadings, like key issues, relevant official documentation, research studies in books and in journals, and vignettes from your school experience. Fill in some details under the subheadings and you will have a core of material to shape to a particular examination question. Make a plan of your answer in the examination room and make what you know serve to answer the questions (see Vignette 6.3). Try to produce an informed argument and do not be afraid to say that there are some different viewpoints and some issues on which people have varying views. Name, and if possible date, is acceptable referencing under examination conditions. If you know you have problems with punctuation and spelling try to leave time for a skim through to make sure this technical aspect does not let you down.

Vignette 6.3 Examination – writing everything I can remember about ...

Problem

M felt very nervous in examinations and tended to write everything she knew about big topics rather than allowing the actual question to narrow the focus.

Solution

M needed to reflect on the criteria for success in the examinations. Answering the actual question, supporting opinions with evidence and developing a coherent argument are generally required. Education students are expected also to illustrate their points with relevant examples from their teaching experience.

M was advised to choose some big topics and to subdivide them into the kind of areas covered in seminars and featured in the course booklet. A topic like reading, for example, could be subdivided into initial teaching of reading; resources; assessment of reading. Each of these headings could be written at the top of a sheet of A4, and then some subheadings, such as main issues; official reports (e.g. the National Curriculum Orders and the National Literacy Strategy Framework for Reading); research studies and other books on reading; classroom vignettes.

M was advised to fill in some details under each of the subheadings. Thus, she was prepared not only for the huge area of reading, but also for some more focused aspects.

Taking control of your argument

This chapter has tried to help you plan, focus and reference your work well and to gather the information you need, whether from the library or from the classroom. To produce a very good rather than merely satisfactory piece of work, you need to let your own 'voice' be heard. You need to take the material by the scruff of the neck and make it serve your argument. Be courageous: if you have carried out your research conscientiously and read widely and deeply, you know enough to write in an informed manner about the issues. The plan helps free you to write what you found out and what its significance is. Many students find it best to let the words and ideas flow – however imperfectly at first. The quality of what is written will gain in strength as you become immersed in the task. Then with something tangible in front of you – your first draft – you can make the account scholarly by checking that all your ideas are clearly expressed and that you have made the references to the work of others serve your analysis. The following short anecdote shows the importance of being at the centre of your analysis. Some years ago a student came to me in great distress. He had wordprocessed his dissertation straight on to the computer from his global plan and some brief notes with relevant reference books at his side. Just as he was about to print out, the unthinkable happened. The file was completely lost. He had three days to work up the 10,000-word study from scratch. But, of course, it was not quite from scratch. In fact, he had internalised his argument so that his reading and classroom findings had become part of his way of thinking about the issues. He managed to write the study up within the time allowed, and actually believed he had written a more coherent dissertation because he had to speed up and develop his argument without constant reference to the work of others. No one would recommend anyone go through this student's ordeal – but the situation sharpened his approach and gave him the courage to write from the heart and mind. The external examiner confirmed a first-class grade.

The pains and the pleasures of study – some student conclusions

This chapter has illustrated some of its points with reference to the questionnaire answers of ten students who had each completed a 10,000-word English curriculum study. At the end of the short questions they were asked to comment briefly on the 'pains and pleasures' of study. This chapter concludes with some reflections on the students' often heartfelt final comments on their experience of the work.

The most mentioned 'pains' included difficulties over time management, controlling a lot of material and, in one case, adjusting expectations of unrealistically dramatic improvements in children's work.

Time management presents a challenge at each stage. At the beginning you have to decide when to stop 'reading round your topic' and start writing a draft. P comments thus: 'I found I had a tendency to "over-read" and therefore the sheer volume of references I had became difficult to organise and time-consuming.' L recalls sitting at the computer feeling overwhelmed by both the amount of secondary source material to include and having to integrate the data from the action research in school. The challenge was to control all this by keeping the focusing research question constantly in mind.

Several students remarked that they underestimated the amount of work involved at the last stage when the final draft is prepared; L pointed out that demands of necessary paid work at the weekend and deadlines for a number of courses coming close together caused a tremendously stressful juggling of priorities. C had a minor illness just as time was running out. Last-minute panics and doubts (like – does any of this make sense!) and worries about quality were also mentioned. Nearly everyone wished they had managed their time better as the handing-in date approached. Keeping to a work plan is very important when several major pieces of work have to be completed about the same time. L writes: 'I should have planned to reach certain goals by a set time, and allowed a tutor to evaluate each stage.'

Longer studies make particular demands in controlling the material, especially when empirical findings need to be integrated. The students in this example had written extended essays before, but integrating data from first-hand enquiry with secondary sources was a new challenge. Again, it was keeping to the research question and the global plan that helped.

Being in control of the material enables the writer to communicate the results honestly and clearly. M had to adjust his original aim, which was to show a development in the quality of the response of older primary children to fiction. 'On looking at my data I had to accept that children had not "magically changed" in the short term as a result of my trying out new teaching strategies.' Modest results and subtle attitudinal changes backed up with evidence from the children's talk or writing are realistic and still worthwhile. The feeling of 'I have spent all this time and nothing truly dramatic has occurred' is understandable, but what can reasonably be expected should bring a better perspective.

On the whole, this small group of students felt the pleasures outweighed the pains in completing what was, in one student's words, 'an original, albeit small-scale, piece of research'. L, for example, relished the opportunity to read research studies as background to devising her own approach to working with the children to investigate writing development. There was new point and meaning in ploughing through journal articles. Another appreciated the opportunity to observe and assess children's progress in a focused manner and liked 'being valued as a teacher researcher'. Three students found the sustained work involved in the dissertation linked work with the college tutor, class teacher and children in a particularly fruitful way. P, for example, wrote that this relatively long-term study clinched understandings about how principles and practices could be related.

Perhaps what comes through most in the responses is the students' pleasure in collaboration. Reading and writing are often viewed as solitary activities, but sharing our developing insights with others often helps us reflect more deeply on the issues. Whether your study is a short structured essay with a given title, or a longer work where you have to carve out your own research area, as in the case of the students referred to here, talk with tutor, class teacher, peers and sometimes children energises the work. Let us leave the final comments to three students. On completing her work, P wrote: 'It had been like nurturing a plant from a seedling, watching it grow from strength to strength, and I felt a certain sadness when I had to give it in.' L admitted that 'the final pleasure was binding up the dissertation and handing in the finished study!' and N's heartfelt comment was: 'Once the last page was printed the feeling of joy and elation was like nothing I have ever experienced'.

Acknowledgement

The authors thank the ten students who took the trouble to fill in the questionnaire about their long essays in such helpful detail, often taking up the invitation to annotate their responses, and Rochelle Lissack who allowed us to quote from her first year (1997) essay.

References

Bell, J. (1987) *Doing Your Research Study*, Milton Keynes: Open University Press.

Bell, J. (1993) *Doing Your Research Project*, second edition, Buckingham: Open University Press.

Cherrington, V. (1990) 'Information books', in B. Wade (ed.) *Reading for Real*, Milton Keynes: Open University Press.

Crystal, D. (1987) *The Cambridge Encyclopaedia of Language*, Cambridge: Cambridge University Press.

Czerniewska, P. (1992) *Learning about Writing*, Oxford: Blackwell.

Department for Education (1995) *English in the National Curriculum*, London: HMSO.

Department for Education (1997) *Initial Teacher Training National Curriculum for Primary English*, London: Teacher Training Agency.

Department for Education and Employment (1998) *The National Literacy Strategy: Framework for Teaching*, London: DfEE.

Hall, N. and Robinson, A. (eds) (1996) *Learning about Punctuation*, Clevedon/Philadelphia/Adelaide: Multilingual Matters.

Hanks, P. (ed.) (1989) *Collins School Dictionary*, Glasgow: Collins.

Language Matters (1995/6) 'Writing', 3 (special edition).

Lunzer, E. and Gardner, K. (1979) *The Effective Use of Reading*, London: Heinemann.

McArthur, T. (1992) *The Oxford Companion to the English Language*, Oxford: Oxford University Press.

Mallett, M. (1992) *Making Facts Matter; Reading Non-fiction 5–11*, London: Paul Chapman.

Moore, P.J. and Scevak, J.J. (1997) 'Learning from texts and visual aids: a developmental perspective', *Journal of Research in Reading* 20, 3: 205–23.

United Kingdom Reading Association (UKRA) (1999) *Reading* 33 (April).

Wade, S.E., Trathen, W. and Schraw, G. (1990) 'An analysis of spontaneous study strategies', *Reading Research Quarterly* 25: 147–66.

Wells, G. (1986) *The Meaning Makers: Children Learning Language and Using Language to Learn*, London: Hodder and Stoughton.

Wray, D. and Lewis, M. (1997) *Extending Literacy: Children Reading and Writing Non-fiction*, London: Routledge.

Wray, D. and Medwell, J. (1997) *English for Primary Teachers*, London: Letts.

APPENDIX 6.1

The questionnaire on the English curriculum 10,000-word dissertation filled in by the ten BA(Ed.) English students.

Please tick your preferred response unless otherwise indicated.

1 Which of the following comes closest to how you selected your chosen topic?
   - (a) something of interest came up on teaching practice;
   - (b) you wanted to research something you knew too little about;
   - (c) you already had an interest in a topic and wanted to find out more.

Comments:

2 Once you had chosen your main area of interest, which of the following did you find most helpful in identifying a focus? Indicate in order of preference – 1, 2, 3, 4, 5:
  (a) talking with a tutor;
  (b) talking with other students;
  (c) brainstorming on your own with a sheet of A4;
  (d) researching in the library;
  (e) discussing the possibilities with the class teacher you were to work with in school.

Comments:

3
  (a) Was the English curriculum dissertation easier or more difficult than the subject English study?

Comments:

  (b) Was the short language essay easier than the English curriculum study?

Comments:

4 Comment on anything you learnt about time management, referencing and general organisation.

5 The dissertation could be replaced by three shorter pieces of work. Please comment.

6 Please indicate by putting 1, 2, 3, 4 which of the following helped most with the dissertation:
   (a) tutor checking through global structure plan;
   (b) tutorials to reflect on the issues in the topic;
   (c) tutor checking through chapter drafts and sending them back with comments;
   (d) other.

Comment on what else might have helped.

7 Please write on the back of this sheet anything you would like to on: (a) the pains, and (b) the pleasures in your journey towards completing your English curriculum study.

Thank you very much for your help.

7 Using information and communications technology

John Jessel

Information and communications technology (ICT) can range from relatively established forms such as tape-recorders, video and television, to more recently developed computer-based facilities such as the wordprocessor, hypertext and the internet. Over the last few years, however, the development of the computer has allowed the use of these different forms of media to become more integrated. For example, photographs taken with a digital camera can be stored in the same way as any other file on disk and fed straight into a computer and included as part of a wordprocessed document. Similarly, audio and video material can be captured, edited and stored as data for research, or used as part of an authored document. The term 'multimedia' is widely used and carries with it connotations about the capability of a computer to handle such ingredients as text, sound, static and moving images. However, such a term says more about the incapability of older computers in the above respects. Indeed, Heppell (1994) regards the term 'multimedia' as potentially redundant, in that everyday life is a multimedia experience but we do not find it necessary to describe it as that.

For the purposes of studying, ICT can be thought of in terms of its possible uses rather than as a copious list of technological devices. ICT can act as a 'tool' which can help you to collect, record and represent data in a variety of ways. Wordprocessors, spreadsheet and other data-handling software, including statistical packages, can facilitate a variety of numerical and administrative tasks. The same software can also provide a means of modelling, or working out ideas. ICT can, of course, also allow material in a variety of forms to be widely distributed and accessed; encyclopaedias on CD-ROMs are commonplace, as are a variety of other learning resources. The internet also allows access to a variety of material as well as allowing people to communicate over long distances.

It is likely that you are already aware of, and will have used, many of the above facilities, and no attempt will be made to cover them all in detail. What will be attempted, however, is a discussion of the impact upon the process of studying of some of the emerging and more widely used ICT applications, such as hypertext and the World Wide Web. These are now briefly introduced before some of the issues and associated study strategies are considered.

Accessing information and resources: hypertext, CD-ROMs and the World Wide Web

Recent developments in technology mean that vast quantities of information can be stored and easily accessed on a world-wide scale. The internet and the CD-ROM (and, more recently, various forms of 'digital versatile disk' such as the DVD-ROM with significantly greater capacity than the CD-ROM) are widely used for distributing information in such forms as text, pictures, animations, sound and movie sequences. The internet is a world-wide network of computers. You may already use it to send messages by e-mail and, perhaps more notably, obtain information and a variety of resources using applications such as the World Wide Web or 'file transfer protocol' (FTP), which allows files to be copied from or to another computer. Access to information on CD-ROMs or the Web is usually through some form of hypertext system where links can be made between any items or pages of stored information. As a user, you might begin by selecting a topic from an index, typically presented as words or in a pictorial form, by using a mouse to point and click over a chosen item. Further information would then appear from which you could make yet another selection, and so on. Information can also be found by typing in the name of a topic so that items deemed to be associated are searched for. Hypertext is easy to use. In general it is obvious where links can be found on a page; these are often shown by pictures or icons, and also by underlined or highlighted words within a body of text. Regardless of whether you use hypertext on the World Wide Web or on a CD-ROM, the methods of access are largely the same. With CD-ROMs the main issue is the limited capacity: this is particularly noticeable with pictures and sound sequences which require a lot of storage space. For the internet there are limitations in terms of access time; for example, large detailed colour images can take many minutes to appear.

The World Wide Web

The Web is made up of vast number of 'pages' of information contained in many computers which are spread around the globe. Pages can consist of text, a variety of graphics, video or sound. Some pages may also allow access to programs and other files which you can copy or 'download' on to your computer. Each page can be accessed using an address, rather like a telephone number, and pages may also be linked to each other using hypertext links. At present, the system has many technical imperfections; websites break down, some pages do not appear or take a long time to appear. Pages may not be accessible when websites are very busy. The internet has had a history of being overloaded and frustratingly slow; however, this could change markedly as methods of transmission are subject to continual and intensive development.

If your computer is connected to the internet and has a piece of software known as a 'browser', then there are a number of ways to access a web page or the collection of pages that make up a website. First, if you have the address for a web page you can simply type this in to view the page. In practice this is tedious because addresses are often lengthy and have to be typed accurately. However, most browsers allow you to store a list of addresses which you can call up. Second, and perhaps more commonly, most browsers will prompt you to access one of a number of search tools. These appear as web pages which usually allow you either to type the name of a topic of your own choice so that it can find a list of associated pages, or to select a topic from a directory of subject headings. Search tools can be broadly categorised into two groups: first, 'search engines' which automatically look for any web pages meeting your search criteria; and second, directories or gateways where there has been some kind of manual selection of pages according to certain standards.

Because there are numerous pages likely to be associated with a given topic, you may, if using a directory, encounter a number of subdirectories before finally accessing a related web page. If you type in a topic for a search then you will be presented with a list of pages which can often run into many thousands. In view of this some issues with regard to study can arise. First, it should be remembered that the internet is not a centrally organised or co-ordinated entity. Anyone can make web pages available and withdraw them at will. There is no control on the nature, quality or accuracy of what is contained on a page. For a start this means that some of the pages that you try to access will no longer exist and you may get some kind of 'error' message instead. It also means that when you use a search engine you may regard many of the pages which are found as spuriously associated. For example, if you type in 'Vikings' with the intention of finding something on the Scandinavian invaders some ten centuries ago, you may instead come across addresses to countless web pages carrying details of match results or press commentaries of a well-known American sports team, or advertising literature of hotels or travel companies bearing the same name. Fortunately, it is possible to narrow down a search by specifying that a page should relate to more than one search word. How this is done may vary from one search engine to another, but most have help pages which are easy to follow. For example, typing in 'Vikings AND Scandinavian' narrows a search, while 'Vikings OR Scandinavian' widens it. Other 'Boolean operators' (named after the nineteenth-century mathematician George Boole), such as FOLLOWED BY, NOT and NEAR, are also typically available. These can be combined and further search conditions specified by the use of parentheses: for example, 'Vikings AND (Scandinavian NEAR invaders)'. Finding relevant web pages often requires patience and ingenuity. It helps to be clear about precisely what information you want. You may need to try different words, or even use a phrase as a search item: for example "zone of proximal development" – the use of double quotes generally being the convention. Repeated attempts and modifications of your search strategy are often required.

Some education authorities, universities, government organisations, radio and television broadcast companies, newspapers, museums, art galleries, publishers and a variety of benevolent organisations provide material they deem educationally relevant and may also provide and maintain lists of selected websites. The pages may be designed to be viewed, or read off the screen, or may contain longer documents or reports which can be downloaded and printed out. Complete texts such as classic novels, philosophical treatises and Shakespeare's works can be obtained and used as data which, for example, can be searched for occurrences of particular words and phrases. Textual or numerical data can also be obtained in spreadsheet format: for example, social and economic statistics, the weather, and performance figures for schools. The contents of web pages can be stored and, if necessary, incorporated into your own work. You may also want to select parts of various pages or download various resources as a form of electronic note-taking. However, the ease of transfer and use of information available on the internet raises issues of copyright, plagiarism and other forms of abuse. It is not unknown for students to include substantial amounts of material from other sources and submit this as their own work. Furthermore, the existence of agencies that supply essay material students can purchase and submit is also widely known.

Once you have access to the internet the financial cost of obtaining information amounts to very little. Many providers offer free services. While much useful material can be obtained, the results of a search can often be disappointing. Although you may find information that is relevant to your area of interest, the content may be out of date and minimal, or the treatment superficial. Sometimes it may help to note who has authored or published the page and to consider the possible motives for the information being there. For example, some advertisers may begin a page with an apparently serious and informative text which can soon give way to details on various products or services. Often material is published by individual enthusiasts whose treatment of a topic may be far from rigorous and may not follow such academic conventions as acknowledging sources or referring to appropriate evidence when necessary. While it may be obvious that some pages are of good quality and others of questionable quality, in many instances particular demands will nevertheless be made on your study skills with regard to the critical scrutiny and use of web pages.

Compact discs and digital versatile discs

The compact disc (CD) and digital versatile disc (DVD) are no more than inexpensive and convenient forms of bulk storage. Compact discs are typically available in a read-only memory (ROM) form where, as the term suggests, you can read what is already stored but not change or add to what is there. Some types of CD can, with a suitable disc-drive, be recorded or 'written' on to, but these are not usually supplied with stored material and in many respects can be regarded as a large-capacity version of a conventional blank floppy disc. The DVD, as well as being of considerably larger capacity that the CD, is more widely available in a writable rather than read-only form. While various titles are currently available in DVD format, the ability to write or record on to the disc has, at the time of writing, yet to be extensively exploited for educational purposes.

CD-ROMs and DVDs can contain anything from software such as a wordprocessor which can be installed on a computer to large volumes of data prepared so that, for example, it is ready to use with a spreadsheet. CD-ROMs often contain a variety of learning resources such as tutorial programs, collections of pictures, simulations and encyclopaedias, where information is organised and can be accessed through hypertext links. In principle, the types of resources can be the same as those found on the internet. In practice, however, because the method of funding is more transparent, it is easier to find material on a CD-ROM or DVD which is the result of a genuine attempt to produce a substantial educational resource, rather than material which exists in relation to some other motive, such as being part of an elaborate advertising ploy. When using CD-ROMs or DVDs you are also less likely to waste time with spurious or non-existent links that characterise the Web.

Learning in hyperspace

Interactivity

The extensive use of hypertext links in World Wide Web pages and CD-ROMs allows you to browse, or follow your own path through the 'hyperspace' created by whatever material is available. You are not constrained by the conventionally fixed sequence of words or events that you are likely to come across in a book or with other media such as television or video. The ability to make choices or decisions and to enter commands or data when using hypertext has been assumed to provide a basis for learning which has been regarded as 'interactive' – you can feel more in control (Race and Brown 1995). Terms such as 'interactive multimedia' and 'interactive CD' are frequently used. More often than not, the connotation is that interactivity is in some way beneficial to learning. Coupled with this is the sense of attractiveness offered by graphics, sound and animation (Maddux 1996). In Chapter 1 the importance of taking a mentally active role in one's learning is argued. Through taking action one can begin to develop more abstract or formal concepts in ways that are meaningful. There are, however, different ways of interacting. At a mentally superficial level you can click a mouse button so that a new page becomes visible, or to set a sound or video sequence in motion. Aldrich *et al.* (1998) draw attention to this kind of interactivity which can be undertaken aimlessly. This can occur with many CD-ROMs which are marketed in terms of their educational value and, regardless of sound and video or other technological capability, are poorly constructed and 'offer little more than light entertainment' (ibid.: 321).

Some tutorial programs aim to convey or 'transmit' a body of information and, every so often, test one's recall of it, and the scope for interaction may be confined to entering responses which are judged as correct or incorrect. Here, a 'reactive' model of interactivity can prevail where learning is framed in quantitative rather than qualitative terms – in effect the drill and practice routine characteristic of the behaviourist approach and subject to the limitations outlined in Chapter 1.

As a result of their work with teachers evaluating CD-ROMs, Aldrich *et al.* (1998) have identified a range of interactivities and how these support various kinds of learning; these are summarised in Table 7.1. At one level the idea is to direct 'attention to key components that are useful or essential for different stages of a problem-solving or a learning task' (ibid.: 329–30). This can be achieved through simulating an aspect of life or the world around us: for example, an animated diagram of how the heart pumps, or a visible representation of the molecules involved in a chemical reaction. These examples of simulations can be contrasted with those which exploit the potential of the computer to respond to your actions. Very often, relatively complex sets of rules may be used so that a range of factors can be linked and this can lead to highlighting the complexities of a topic (Robertson 1998). For example, you could be required to adopt the role of a decision-maker, such as a headteacher, and take various courses of action to deal with a problem such as balancing the school budget, or improving pupil discipline. In these cases the consequences of your actions would be fed back, and this in turn could set further constraints which you would have to deal with. Simulations of this kind allow you to explore how a variety of factors might interact; rather than being a case of entering right or wrong answers, the idea is to provide a starting point for exploring and discussing a set of issues. Aldrich *et al.* (1998) use the term 'experimentation and testing' to include running simulations which can be used, for example, to test the effects of pollution on a given eco-system. Simulations of this nature, of course, have their dangers in that they can oversimplify the complexities of real life, and this can lead to false perceptions. Also, a common criticism is that simulations can be very abstract, devoid of context and not easy to use.

In contrast to using a ready-made model that exists within a simulation, you can build your own model and compare how it performs with 'real life' observations. Although there is scope for complexity, much can be gained from building a comparatively simple model representing some aspect of a situation, in that you can take a more active role as a learner and develop your own mental models. Modelling can be carried out in many ways on the computer; although customised programs exist, more familiar applications such as spreadsheets and drawing packages can be used: for example, a spreadsheet for modelling a school budgeting system, and a drawing package to represent and manipulate objects in a room so that an overall layout can be experimented with.

Interactivity can involve transforming information, and in this way can be linked with the idea of generative study strategies introduced in Chapter 1. Modelling is an example of this. However, understanding can also be developed by making changes to, or adapting existing material for your own purposes. This is consistent with the 'manipulability and annotatability' dimension of interactivity suggested by Aldrich *et al.* (ibid.). A further development is their dimension of 'creativity and combinability', where new representations can be constructed by using and combining different media. Here a variety of tools such

Table 7.1 Dimensions for assessing the interactivity of CD-ROMs

Visibility and accessibility

- visualise content in different ways (e.g. the invisible made visible);
- access content in different ways (e.g. multiple views of the same topic).

Manipulability and annotatability

- construct content (e.g. make a new food web);
- make notes.

Creativity and combinability

- create new content by combining media (e.g. making a multimedia document by recording sounds, building animations).

Experimentation and testing

- run a simulation;
- build a model.

Source: Aldrich *et al.* 1998, p. 331. © BECTA.

as the wordprocessor, desktop publisher, spreadsheets and graphing software, data-handling software, music, graphics and animation packages might be used.

Information in fragments

A convenient page size for most hypertext documents is the computer screen. However, a computer screen has its limitations – particularly when it comes to reading large volumes of text. Although the size and resolution of computer screens may vary, and pages larger than the screen may be scrolled through, the same basic design principles for a hypertext page still apply. These take into account how much text can be presented, and that pages should have a visual impact. The motivating effects of stimulating visual imagery and colour have been frequently argued (e.g. Brown and Knight 1994). It is also widely held that 'condensing information into succinct, precise statements or questions becomes an essential art for computer-based learning designers' (Race and Brown 1995: 71). Although the above factors can make learning from hypertext appear to be an attractive proposition, some criticisms have been voiced. For example, Whalley (1993) regards hypertext as fragmented, and Mühlhäuser (1992) regards the degree of freedom offered in terms of the number of possible routes through documents as leading to 'anarchistic' computer-based learning systems. However, diSessa (1988) argues that much of our intuitive knowledge gained from everyday experience is fragmented in nature, and that such fragments can be built upon and integrated through the use of computers. Wolf (1988) also acknowledges that while much of what we know is the result of piecing together fragments from the past, or fragments arising from our own observations in the present, there is also a social dimension to this. This social or 'discursive' dimension is made explicit by Harré and Gillett (1994: 22) who regard 'the mind as the meeting point of a wide range of structuring influences whose nature can only be painted on a broader canvas than that provided by the study of individual organisms'. It is not the individual who is trying to make sense of the pieces to solve a problem, but a community within which expertise is shared. If hypertext can allow links to be made between minds then a discursive element in learning can occur by this means.

Megarry (1995) contrasts hypertext with the more conventional linear form of text in a book. Linear text is structured and organised to assist a dialogue with the reader. A 'story' or 'narrative' can transcend a printed text and, as Plowman (1996) argues, provide a global coherence which can aid both comprehension and recall. In constructivist terms, the narratives conveyed by such means as printed text, lectures and television provide organising structures. Although narratives can communicate content in the Vygotskian sense (see Chapter 1) by placing the learner in the role of a listener, Laurillard (1995) argues that 'telling the story' may not always work effectively; there are times when alternatives are needed which give more control to the learner. However, allowing the learner complete autonomy to interact may mean a significant departure from a narrative, or organising framework. While this can be successful for the 'expert scholar' it can be chancy for someone less expert who is tackling a new area. One way of reconciling this has been suggested by Laurillard (ibid.); she argues that hypertext documents can be designed so that as a learner you can have a measure of control, and be encouraged both to interact through investigating data and to provide your own analysis and commentary, but that you can also have access to the author's narrative line or analyses for means of comparison. This could reduce the probability of aimless wandering through unfathomable material. However, many hypertexts do not have these suggested qualities, and a key issue as a learner is taking cognitive action on what is otherwise no more than a collection of data in a variety of forms. Thomas (1997) suggests that one's own interests can provide an organising and guiding framework. This could be important if the narrative or other means of organisation characteristic of conventional forms of text is not in evidence.

In view of the above issues, and on a more practical level, when using hypertext for studying it may be advantageous for browsing to be approached purposefully. In this case it is important to keep your more central questions and interests in mind and use pages selectively, rather than be lured away by attractive links which may be of only passing interest. Purposeful browsing can be thought of as a form of active reading and in keeping with the constructivist principles introduced in Chapter 1. However, in comparison to a book, a hypertext document is difficult to scan for key headings and other features which can give an overall sense of what is there, providing a holistic framework which can help understanding. Although indexes can help, when you move from one hypertext page to another these may no longer be visible or easily accessible. Also, when using a book you can easily glance back and forth to recap or see what is coming next; however, the original words on the computer screen disappear (Race and Brown 1995), and again this can also compromise active reading strategies.

The use of hypertext for studying does not, of course, preclude the use of material in other forms. Megarry (1995) argues that books have an important and continuing role: 'hypermedia does not – and never will – replace books and print: it invites a new relationship, in which print is reinvented and celebrated afresh' (ibid. : 146). The use of the term 'multimedia' in association with hypertext might suggest that the latter can easily and effectively lend itself to the transmission of a variety of material including books or documents already existing in other forms. While this may be a technical possibility it may not always work effectively; careful design may need to be built into a hypertext document at the outset, drawing on its distinctive qualities. In some contexts a hypertext document may not be a clearly definable entity and coherence in design may be compromised. When using hypertext on the internet you are likely to access not one discrete text but a web of interrelated texts. The distinction between one author and another can become blurred. Furthermore, the possibility of editing existing texts and the links between them also blurs the distinction between author and reader (Thomas 1997). The issues arising from the proliferation of hypertext through such vehicles as CD-ROMs, DVDs and the World Wide Web are extensive, and the nature of literacy, or 'information literacy', and the study practices associated with it, are open to change.

Working at a distance

E-mail facilities are provided within most universities and schools. More usefully, perhaps, they can be set up at home or anywhere else convenient where a computer can be linked via a modem to a telephone system. Lists of e-mail addresses can be easily stored and a copy of the same mail can be sent to a number of people simultaneously. In effect, you send mail from your computer to the computer belonging to your e-mail service provider, where in turn it is relayed from one computer to another until it arrives at the computer belonging to the service provider of the person you are sending the mail to. The mail then sits and waits so that it can be read when the recipient logs into their mailbox. The relaying process can take place almost at once, although when sending to more distant parts of the world it can take several hours. If you are using a modem link and your service provider is local, then the telephone cost is no more than for any other local call of the same duration, and the charge made by a service provider is usually minimal or free. In practice, if messages are longer than a few words it may be advantageous to prepare text in advance, for example as a wordprocessed document which can be copied into the e-mail window and sent. More sophisticated electronic mail facilities allow computer files, such as wordprocessed essays, to be sent as an 'attachment' and the person receiving them can read them, provided they have compatible software. In principle any computer file can be sent as an attachment: for example, desktop published documents, music files, sound samples and video clips. Essays of several thousand words may take a few seconds to send, while anything containing graphics or sound, which usually take up more storage space, can take several minutes or more.

E-mail allows you to work at a distance; you can help, or get help from, other students and liaise with tutors. It is quite common for writing to be sent and returned with comments this way. Similarly, it is possible to prepare work collaboratively using e-mail. An extension of the e-mail idea is termed 'computer conferencing'. In practice this is rather like an electronic notice board where anyone belonging to a conferencing group can pin electronic messages for anyone else in the group to look at. Although there are dedicated conferencing packages which make it easier to organise your own and others' contributions, conventional e-mail software can serve the purpose. Any group of people with access to e-mail can organise themselves into a conference group. However, the group is usually set up in relation to a particular project rather than, say, an ongoing interest, and conferencing takes place over a relatively limited period of time, such as a few weeks or even a few days. In practice, rather like a chaired debate, it can help if one person acts as a co-ordinator, encouraging contributions when necessary and helping to keep a focus. Unlike face-to-face conversation, feedback in a computer conference is unlikely to be immediate; there is time to reflect on contributions before making one's own.

Another variation of electronic communication which allows people to share information is the newsgroup. Many service providers allow access to a variety of newsgroups which, unlike conferences, exist for indefinite periods of time. Newsgroups are usually organised by topic and can relate to anything from the interests or obsessions of enthusiasts to a variety of professional interests. Rather like World Wide Web pages, though, the quality and the extent to which they are maintained can, of course, vary enormously.

As with e-mail, remote access to academic libraries via the internet is almost routine. Perhaps most useful is the facility to search library catalogues; however, reservations and renewals are usually possible. Bibliographic searches of databases containing details of a variety of texts, including abstracts of academic journal articles, are also well established on the Web, and details on how to access these can be obtained from many libraries or information service centres.

It has been argued that electronic communication increases the possibilities for study at a time and place of one's own choosing (Darby 1995). Darby also notes the possibility of enrolling on courses at a distance; one might even choose and assemble modules from a variety of providers world-wide, and any image of a course being dominated by sitting for hours in a lecture theatre is automatically challenged. Furthermore, one can gain from the perspectives offered by working with students and tutors from many countries. In Chapter 1 the importance of social factors in learning is highlighted. Although these can take effect solely by electronic means, in some subject areas tutors who organise courses place importance upon face-to-face encounters and practical experience. The extent and the way in which electronic communities develop remains to be seen. For the moment, knowing people electronically can be regarded as an additional experience rather than a replacement, and presents another aspect of being a student.

Wordprocessing

If you use a computer then it is likely that the use of the wordprocessor will feature extensively within your study activities. Even if you do not use a wordprocessor as such, many other computer applications, such as hypertext authoring software and desktop publishers, allow text to be entered and edited. Through editing text, you can work through and represent your ideas, and it is upon this aspect of wordprocessing that I will now briefly focus.

Writing can involve a lot more than unloading the contents of your memory on to paper. On some occasions you will know what you want to say and how you will express it in words. At other times writing will form part of the process of discovering what you want to say. As part of this process you will be reconstructing ideas and making your own connections between ideas in a way which will often be unique to the piece of writing that you produce. In this sense study is a creative process. In Chapter 1 it is pointed out that noting down ideas helps unburden the memory so that we can more easily revise and build upon our thoughts. When you begin a piece of writing you may have some idea of the topic you are going to write about but may be unsure as to exactly what you want to say, which points will be important, which points can be discarded and how your ideas can be linked to form an overall narrative or argument. At this stage it may be helpful just to type in odd words or phrases which represent a collection of initial ideas as they occur to you. At this 'brainstorming' phase it may be more important to keep the flow of ideas going before subjecting them to critical scrutiny or removal. You may wish to use pen and paper in conjunction with the wordprocessor, particularly for overall mapping, where graphic elements such as connecting lines may help. As you begin to group and order ideas, you may find your use of the wordprocessor begins to take over as you expand the fragments of text into more coherent points. Here, of course, unlike working with pen and paper, your final copy will not have to be retyped from scratch. At some later stage you can reflect more carefully on your choice of words, and whether you think they represent your ideas accurately and how clear they may be to others.

There can sometimes be a very large gap between what you think you are saying and the way this is understood by the reader. Rather than assuming that what you write is a clear incontrovertible message, it is often helpful to consider your writing as merely a collection of words and that any message arises from the reader's interpretation of those words. How your words are interpreted, like any other perceptual process, will be influenced by a reader's current thoughts and past experiences, and these may be very different to your own at the time of writing. In view of this it sometimes helps to detach yourself from your writing by leaving a gap of time before re-reading and revising your work critically.

In essence, all of the above processes are part of redrafting. Redrafting in the fullest sense means working with ideas both at sentence level and in terms of the overall argument or structure. It may only be at a relatively late stage in your writing that you begin to look at details such as typing errors, spelling and grammar. These final presentational details, although important, can interrupt your thoughts and impede your writing if you are over-preoccupied with them at the start. In sum, it may be seldom that you approach your writing as a sequence from beginning to end. To take a simple example, your introductory paragraphs may be the last ones that you write, because initially you may not be sure what will be written. Redrafting, like any other process, has its dangers; you can keep on moving bits of text around until what is being written loses overall balance, coherence and spontaneity. In view of this, you will need to keep a perspective on the main points of what you want to say.

New kinds of authorship

In addition to becoming readers of hypertext documents on CD-ROMs and websites, we may also make our contribution as 'writers' or authors. In the same way that essays and other forms of continuous prose are routinely produced as part of study activity, hypertext authoring could play a larger role. Work assignments, in both schools and colleges, are increasingly requiring the use of a range of ICT tools, including the use of hypertext. *The Requirements for Courses of Initial Teacher Training* (DfEE 1998), for example, makes frequent reference to the interactivity of ICT systems and their use in presenting information in ways suitable for different audiences. Increasingly both individuals and institutions are setting up their own websites. In view of the issues concerning the form of information conveyed by hypertext and the model of reading that this implies, one might consider whether a new kind of literacy is demanded. In turn, the medium of presentation may also have implications for what kind of material people may seek.

Being able to exploit the potential of hypertext fully means that, in addition to entering and making connections between blocks of written text, you will need to be able to use a variety of tools which embrace a variety of multimedia components. For example, as an author you would be rather limited if you wished to include an image in a hypertext document and did not know how to capture, create or manipulate that image. Using hypertext, then, also means being able to use such facilities as drawing and electronic paint packages, scanners, digital photographic cameras, a range of other peripherals and software for manipulating sound, music and animation sequences. As computers become more capable and responsive these tools are becoming both more available and easier to use.

New technology opens up new possibilities for representing ideas and for creativity. We can experiment with transforming or representing ideas in other forms. In particular our generative study strategies could more regularly involve thinking visually. In Chapter 1 it is suggested that learning can be viewed in terms of the development of mental structures. The idea of generative study strategies is applied to the act of using existing knowledge and abilities to transform information and ideas and represent ideas in a variety of forms. The use of hypertext can make generative demands both in terms of the different forms of representation which it can incorporate and in terms of the arrangement of the elements within it. In particular, such higher-order thinking and information-handling skills as classifying, decision-making and organising can be encouraged (Pritchard 1996). The relationships which can be explored and worked with between pictures and text or, more generally, between any comprising elements of a piece of work can lead to deeper understanding and, as is often observed, to a sense of making knowledge your own. Recognising when to use the variety of ICT tools that are available may not happen automatically, particularly if we are part of a culture which has hitherto been linearly verbal rather than visual. The impact of ICT and the associated forms of literacy on study raises some interesting questions for the future.

References

Aldrich, F., Rogers, Y. and Scaife, M. (1998) 'Getting to grips with "interactivity": helping teachers assess the educational value of CD-ROMs', *British Journal of Educational Technology* 29, 4: 321–32.

Brown, S. and Knight, P. (1994) *Assessing Learners in Higher Education*, London: Kogan Page.

Darby, J. (1995) 'Education in the year 2000: Will we recognise it?', in F. Percival, R. Land and D. Edgar-Nevill (eds) *Aspects of Education and Training Technology XXVIII. Computer Assisted and Open Access Education*, London: Kogan Page.

Department for Education and Employment (DfEE) (1998) *Circular number 4/98. Requirements for Courses of Initial Teacher Training*, London: DfEE.

diSessa, A.A. (1988) 'Knowledge in pieces', in G. Forman and P.B. Pufall (eds) *Constructivism in the Computer Age*, Hillsdale, NJ: Lawrence Erlbaum Associates.

Harré, R and Gillett, G. (1994) *The Discursive Mind*, Thousand Oaks, California: SAGE Publications.

Heppell, S. (1994) 'Multimedia and learning: normal children, normal lives and real change', in J.D.M. Underwood (ed.) *Computer Based Learning: Potential into Practice*, London: David Fulton.

Laurillard, D. (1995) 'Multimedia and the changing experience of the learner', *British Journal of Educational Technology* 26, 3: 179–89.

McAleese, R. (1993) 'Navigation and browsing in hypertext', in R. McAleese (ed.) *Hypertext: Theory into Practice*, Oxford: Intellect Books.

Maddux, C. (1996) 'The state of the art in Web-based learning', *Computers in Schools* 12, 4: 63–71.

Megarry, J. (1995) 'Paradoxes in hypermedia: design, support and training', in F. Percival, R. Land and D. Edgar-Nevill (eds) *Aspects of Education and Training Technology XXVIII. Computer Assisted and Open Access Education*, London: Kogan Page.

Mühlhäuser, M. (1992) 'Hypermedia and navigation as a basis for authoring/learning environments', *Journal of Educational Multimedia and Hypermedia* 1, 1: 51–64.

Plowman, L. (1996) 'Narrative, linearity and interactivity: making sense of interactive multimedia, *British Journal of Educational Technology* 27, 2: 92–105.

Pritchard, A. (1996) 'Schema theory and the use of hypertext-style computer programs', *British Journal of Educational Technology* 27, 3: 233–6.

Race, P. and Brown, S. (1995) 'Getting the wording right', in F. Percival, R. Land and D. Edgar-Nevill (eds) *Aspects of Education and Training Technology XXVIII. Computer Assisted and Open Access Education*, London: Kogan Page.

Robertson, J. (1998) 'Paradise lost: children, multimedia and the myth of interactivity', *Journal of Computer Assisted Learning* 14: 31–9.

Thomas, H. (1997) 'The New Literacy?: The challenges of hypertextual discourse', *Computer Assisted Language Learning* 10, 5: 479–89.

Whalley, P. (1993) 'An alternative rhetoric for hypertext', in C. McKnight, A. Dillon and J. Richardson (eds) (1993) *Hypertext: a Psychological Perspective*. Chichester: Ellis Horwood.

Wolf, D.P. (1988) 'The quality of interaction: domain knowledge, social interchange, and computer learning', in G. Forman and P. B. Pufall (eds) *Constructivism in the Computer Age*, Hillsdale, NJ: Lawrence Erlbaum Associates.

8 Presenting your work orally

Jenny Griffiths

Introduction

You have been asked to make an oral presentation of some kind. Whether it is of a formal or an informal nature, you need to give the activity some thought and preparation if you are to avoid 'the abysmal quality of many presentations' (Robson 1993: 422). Presenting your work in this way is not an easy option; indeed, for many, the pressures that are engendered can seem almost overwhelming.

To help gauge students' feelings about giving an oral presentation a short questionnaire was devised (see Appendix 8.1). The following quotes come from the responses to that survey. For many of the students the most worrying aspects were:

> 'knowing what I want to say and not being able to find the words'
>
> 'having my mind go blank!!!'
>
> 'getting my ideas and words muddled up'
>
> 'leaving out important information'
>
> 'drying up and making a complete fool of myself'

These states of insecurity may go some way towards explaining the high proportion of individuals who place having to make a presentation as among the most traumatic experiences they could undergo, certainly far more distressing than having to complete an essay. So why might this be?

A written piece of work presents many challenges but at least it can be fashioned in privacy, honed to a good standard of content and presentation and then submitted. The writer is safe in the knowledge that the words are not going to move around on the page or the neatly typed text transform itself into an indecipherable scrawl. The individual making an oral presentation, however, often feels they can have no such sureties about their material. The nightmare of words jumbling themselves up or the content being so muddled as to be incomprehensible can haunt the speaker's thoughts and undermine their confidence.

This chapter sets out to highlight ways in which the process can be managed successfully. Through gaining some insight into why you experience feelings which may range from mild anxiety to full-blown panic, you can develop a measure of self-awareness regarding these which Goleman (1996: 47) suggests is 'a first step in gaining some control'. In addition, a range of other strategies will be considered through which the individual can take some control of the whole oral presentation process. As you may have seen from other chapters in this book, how we go about processes such as reading, writing or oral presentation varies from individual to individual. This chapter offers you examples of ways others have found helpful which can enable you to gain some understanding of your own preferred methods of working. The cohort of students who produced the 'worrying' quotes above also completed a short feedback sheet after their presentations had taken place (see Appendix 8.2). The following comments on learning from others are drawn from their ideas of what proved the most helpful strategies for them:

> 'sharing and discussing ideas with others'
>
> 'listening to other people and through this gaining insight into other strategies to use to help yourself'
>
> 'sharing different approaches'
>
> 'giving ideas of ways to present to the rest of your group'

The rest of the chapter will make use of other comments drawn from the questionnaire and feedback to highlight aspects of the presentation process.

In approaching the task of making an oral presentation, whether of a formal or an informal nature, there are many different elements to consider during the period of time from initial preparations through to the presentation itself. These elements fall, with some overlap, into one of three categories; the first two contribute to the structuring of and preparation for the presentation and the third to its successful communication to an audience.

Structuring your presentation

Gathering the material

> 'I found it most helpful to leave enough time to adjust the final product.'

The tried and tested ways of gathering the material for this process echo those used for written work, and you are probably best served using the strategies you find most helpful in the written context. What is important is to recognise that there are aspects of giving an oral presentation which require some preparation in advance if you are to have success. If you are the kind of learner who leaves everything until the last minute and then completes before the deadline on a rush of adrenaline, you need to consider whether, in this case, there are some elements of the process which need to be treated differently from written assignments. An oral presentation often involves more than speaking; for example, it could include visual aids such as handout materials, demonstrations requiring equipment, slides, video or overhead transparencies. These all need time for preparation. In addition, they need to be tied into the verbal element of the presentation, which presupposes that this has been at least mapped out before the visual aids are prepared.

Selecting and shaping

> 'I am concerned about organising the amount of material to suit the time allocated.'

> 'I'd like some help on how to get my point across clearly.'

Having gathered your material, you enter the phase where you select and shape it into a coherent whole for the audience. Perhaps the first thing to bear in mind is that reading and listening are two very different activities. The reader is able to do many things that the listener cannot, the most important of which is perhaps the ability to set their own rate of assimilation of information and ideas. The reader can also go back and examine those ideas again by rereading passages and taking time out to ponder on the questions raised. In addition, while engaging with a small part they can nevertheless still gain some sense of the whole as they hold a body of text in their hands. This offers a context that the reader can access at any point if they so wish. The reader can become, as Jessel points out in Chapter 1, 'mentally active', interacting with the text. When composing an oral presentation, therefore, it is necessary for the speaker to consider the needs of listeners carefully and make provision for them. A comfortable rate of assimilation for the audience is one of the first of these. This rate will vary to some degree with the listeners' familiarity with the material being presented. Having an understanding of 'who your audience is', therefore, is important; it will impact on both what and how much material you offer.

Giving this material a structure which is made explicit to the listeners (signposting) will offer them a sense of control over the content, allowing them to access it more easily. As part of this structure, offering an overview of what the presentation will cover replicates to some extent the experience that a reader gets when holding a book or document. Although the overview and explicit structure go some way to facilitating understanding, your listeners will still not be able to manipulate the material of their own volition. It therefore becomes your responsibility to ensure that ideas are reinforced by a combination of other elements: for example, the use of visual aids, repetition combined with a vivid use of language, rhythm, pattern and the use of the rhetorical question, anecdotes, illustrations and examples, using humour and mixing familiar information with old.

> 'I'm worried about maintaining the interest of the audience.'

This student's concern highlights another reason for using a range of approaches or strategies. Can you remember remaining totally focused on what a speaker was saying for longer than twenty minutes? Listeners tend to take short attention breaks quite frequently during the course of any listening episode. If you are the speaker you need to counteract this. In shaping your material you should take account of the human need for variety in maintaining attention by ensuring aspects of your presentation change at intervals throughout its length. When you are putting your talk together you can build in structural changes, such as dividing the talk into clear sections which you can signal or signpost to the audience and noting points at which you will introduce visual or sound materials. This change in direction acts as a mental 'jolt' to members of your audience, who then find it easier to maintain their interest. At the preparation stage it is vital to structure your talk to try to achieve maximum audience attention.

> 'Being able to cover key elements within a time limit is my worry.'

In composing and structuring your material you need also to take into consideration the amount of time you have available for the presentation. Your listeners will want to feel that you have covered a satisfactorily substantial area, but attempting to cram too much in is counterproductive. You are likely to rush in order to get everything said and your listeners may well feel overwhelmed. Being clear in your own mind about what you want to say and focusing carefully on that is more likely to result in successful coverage which your listeners will appreciate.

> 'I prepared far enough in advance to become familiar with the content.'

Finally, as you build your talk you are also beginning to inhabit the material for yourself. The familiarisation process is an important step in establishing confidence in your ability to successfully present your ideas 'on the day'.

Preparation

> 'I would be most helped by being well prepared.'

Being prepared means having thought of and made provision for both your own and the audience's needs. We begin with thinking about the visual aids that you may decide to use.

Visual aids

> 'I was most helped by practising with the OHP prior to the day.'

> 'I found checking how to use and handle the visual aids and hardware before the day my most helpful strategy.'

The first thing you will want to do is check what facilities for visual aids will be available to you: for example, will there be provision for a flip chart, OHP, slide projector, sound system or video? Once this has been clarified, thought needs to be given at the selecting and shaping stage as to what aids you might use, and why. At which points would it be appropriate to introduce them? What do you want them to do, generate interest, focus attention, clarify a particular point? Which would be the most helpful and manageable to use? Having made these decisions you should then locate these aids or create some of your own. Don't leave this until the last minute. Location and creation can turn out to be time-consuming exercises, and if you are up against a deadline you run the risk of not getting what you want and having to adjust accordingly.

At this stage it is worth giving thought to how you can achieve the best materials possible. Listeners will usually welcome something to look at, but it must aid their understanding otherwise it becomes a source of puzzlement or frustration. If the audience is unable to see the relevance of the visual aid – that is, if they cannot understand how it links with the subject of your presentation – they will tend to switch off from your talk to tussle with the problem of making meaning from what seems a meaningless message. If, on the other hand, they can see that it relates to your argument but is of a quality that makes it difficult to access – for example, the type is too small for those at the back to read – then frustration sets in and you begin to lose their interest.

Full script – cue cards – extemporising

I was most helped by:

> 'writing my speech as I would say it'
>
> 'spending time preparing my prompts beforehand'
>
> 'using my cue cards with key points'
>
> 'ad-libbing from the OHP'

In giving a presentation one has the opportunity to engage with the audience in a way that is impossible through the written medium. A subject can come alive when the speaker's enthusiasm and involvement with the material is allowed to show and is communicated with the listener. The delivery style you choose for your presentation should therefore support you sufficiently to allow you to do this.

In academic contexts, as opposed to many others, there appears to be an assumption that to give a paper or presentation requires only that the speaker stand in front of the assembled listeners and read verbatim from a text which is circulated to all those present. While this may still be the accepted practice on many occasions, it is one that needs to be challenged. If all you are going to do is to give a poor reading of a distributed text, you might as well dispense with the speaker and let the audience get on with reading at their own pace. However, it is possible to work successfully from a full script but it is certainly not an easy option. In order to do a full script justice, it needs to be prepared thoroughly and carefully rehearsed. Even very experienced speakers do this, and if you are just beginning you will certainly need the support this kind of preparation gives. The speech needs to be written in spoken language and laid out in an easily accessible form, with indicators to alert you to such things as what you should emphasise and where you should pause; see Nicholls (1991) for a good introduction to the techniques you can use. If the fully written script is for you, then one word of warning: never allow yourself to spend so long on writing it that you skip the rehearsal stage. Doing this will almost inevitably mean your listeners will get a speaker whose eyes are glued to the printed page and they will be denied the lively and engaging experience they deserve.

You may feel that an entirely written speech will restrict you and prevent you engaging with the listeners as fully as you would like. On the other hand, you know you need some kind of support to help you remember important points and ensure the structure of your talk remains intact. For you, cue cards are probably the answer; they are used successfully by many speakers. They need to be a manageable size for holding comfortably and should be made out of a material that is reasonably robust. Pieces of card are probably ideal, strong enough to take a hole for a tag to hold them in order and easy to turn, too. Each cue card should contain very clear, brief headings or phrases to remind you of the next step in your speech. They can also include other important reminders – to use a particular visual aid, for example – and should be numbered, just in case they are dropped! The writing on them needs to be of a size that you can read easily when they are held at around your waist level. This allows you to manage them discreetly without having to bring them up to normal reading distance where they would begin to come between you and your listeners.

Some people, perhaps those most confident with their material, find that using OHP or flip chart headings provides the structure they need while allowing them the freedom to extemporise. Here the speaker and listeners share the same visual prompts, creating a sense of immediacy that can be very persuasive. It also carries the additional benefit of releasing the speaker's hands, which can then be used to enhance their speech.

Finally, I would not advocate trying to give a presentation of anything longer than a few minutes without some kind of notes or support. Even if you feel very secure in your subject area, you can still find yourself struggling under the pressure of the occasion if you have nothing to fall back on.

Coping with nervousness and stress

Presenting orally, no matter what the context, makes demands of the individual that many find stressful. As students in our survey commented:

> 'It scares me to think about presenting.'
>
> 'I will sweat so much from nerves and feel sick and faint.'

One of your tasks, therefore, is to discover the strategies that enable you to manage your stress in a positive manner. As Coben points out in Chapter 2, stress in itself is not negative. How one manages stress, however, can be. Approaches to try during the preparation period include familiarising oneself with the material to be delivered, relaxation, using mental techniques, and practice.

Familiarisation

> 'I was most helped by practising on members of the family so that the presentation was familiar on the day.'

> 'Preparing my presentation some time before the day helped keep me calm and enabled me to familiarise myself with its content.'

It is probably a mistake to try and learn any talk by heart. Unless you are a consummate actor you will run the risk of sounding stilted and will also reduce your ability to cope flexibly should you need to make any adjustments on the day. In addition, the pressures of memorisation are likely to increase your stress levels rather than reduce them. For most people, preparation of any speech which is not fully scripted will be more helpful if it involves talking about the area of their presentation to anyone who will listen. If you do this, you will be building up a collection of words and phrases around the subject which you can more readily draw on when you come to present. If finding anyone to talk to proves impossible, some people find they can make do with themselves, even if it does feel a little odd.

Relaxation

> 'I think I will be most helped by trying to keep my nerves under control by relaxation.'

Whenever there is a discussion about how speakers can best approach a presentation, you can be sure that the benefits of relaxation will be raised. Those for whom relaxation seems an impossibility usually greet this with some scepticism. There are ways, however, that you can go about developing your ability to relax which have proved successful for others. These methods range from physically active approaches, where you may, for example, stretch, tense or shake muscles or limbs and then allow them to go limp, to those which rely on mental processes alone. The brain controls the body, and mental techniques can involve such activities as visualisation of soothing situations or simply thinking about relaxing particular muscles, which sends signals to them to do so. The secret is to find a method which suits you: that is, one at which you feel you can persevere. Although relaxing the muscles of your body does affect your mental state and can be a powerful weapon in combating nerves, for some people it is not achieved easily. Therefore it is important to give it consideration at the preparation stage while you still have time to do something about it. There are many books that describe a variety of relaxation techniques, and some are listed at the end of this chapter.

Mental techniques

> 'It's important to acknowledge to yourself that you are fearful, and work at moving beyond that fear.'

> 'I was helped by remembering it was only a few minutes of my life.'

Our thoughts are a powerful medium which some of us find easier to harness than others. We are probably aware that, of the people we know, at one extreme there is the individual who appears to be able to take difficulties in their stride, finding ways around most problems, while at the other end there is one who seems to get overwhelmed by events and spends much time sunk in despair. Most of us fall somewhere in between these two extremes. There are those who suggest that part, if not all, of the coping individual's apparent ability to rise above difficulties lies in their tendency to think positively and not allow themselves to dwell on and magnify setbacks (Seligman 1989, Lloyd-Elliot 1991). Wilson (1994: 200) describes how 'self-talk is used by many performers to "psyche themselves up" while others seem to specialize in "talking themselves down"'. A technique such as this may work well for those who tend to be verbalisers in cognitive style (see Chapter 5) but for imagers, who prefer to work in pictures, then perhaps a strategy such as goal imaging (Wilson 1994: 201) will be more successful. Using this technique you use your 'mind's eye' to create a mental film or video of the event during which you perform successfully. This approach has an additional advantage in that there is some evidence from research (Feltz and Landers 1983, Suter 1986) to suggest that skills may be improved simply by imagining you are carrying them out. You will find advice on how to go about developing these kinds of mental techniques in many books on the market aimed at both the performing artist and the non-specialist (see end of chapter).

Practice

> 'Tips and advice were helpful, but I think practice is the only way you can improve presentation skills.'

We come now to a strategy that has a great deal to offer but which many ignore or give low priority. In the survey carried out with undergraduates, fewer than 40 per cent of respondents placed practice (either alone or with peers) as one of their first three preferred options in preparing for the presentation. The giving of a talk demands a large element of skill, and like all skills it has to be practised to be acquired (Hayes 1994). You would not expect to be able to drive a car well, read a book with ease, make a cake with a fair expectation of success, if you had had little if any practice at the skills involved.

> 'I found helpful feedback from colleagues was useful.'

'Knowledge of results is an essential feature of skill learning' (Hayes 1994: 671) so when practising you need feedback to help you gain insight into how the audience is likely to perceive you. The comments of a critical friend can be invaluable at this stage. They will see and hear the things that you are unlikely to notice.

> 'I was helped by practising the presentation until I felt comfortable with it.'

Practice really is the very best way of managing the nerves which all speakers experience when they first start to present. The vast majority continue to feel nervous at the prospect of speaking, particularly when, for example, the subject is new to them or the occasion is an important one. What you need to remember, however, is that a certain level of nervousness has a beneficial effect. It triggers the release of adrenaline into the bloodstream, which in turn causes you to be more alert and able to cope. However, excessive nervousness can lead to such high levels of adrenaline that over-arousal is caused and, linked with it, a marked deterioration in performance. Wilson (1994) points out that in understanding this phenomenon three variables need to be considered:

1 The sensitivity of the individual to negative evaluation and fear of failure.
2 The degree of mastery over the task that has been attained, either through preparation or the lack of it, and the difficulty of the task itself.
3 The degree of social or environmental pressure prevailing at the time, e.g. at an informal meeting or a public performance or examination.

This kind of information can be useful in making decisions about your own likelihood of succumbing to debilitating nerves. It also offers insight into how you might go about mitigating the impact. So, for example, if you think you are particularly sensitive to negative evaluation and fear of failure, you might make extra effort to develop your relaxation techniques so that they can be deployed successfully on the presentation day. On the other hand, you may feel that your original choice of subject matter will be too challenging for you and that you would give a better account of yourself if you chose an area where you felt more secure. As one of the students commented, 'one of the most helpful strategies was talking about a topic on which you felt most confident'. Recognising your particular needs and then taking steps to meet them allows you to feel in control of the experience. This also goes some way towards reducing nervousness.

Care and development of your voice

Your voice is a remarkable instrument, capable of infinite variation which allows it to convey a wide range of thoughts, ideas and feelings. It is unique to you and forms part of who you are. It is created inside you and is therefore very bound up with your body and mind, both of which can affect it for good or ill. It is important, therefore, that physically and mentally you are well prepared for the demands to be made on your voice.

In circumstances such as presentations, where additional pressures come to bear on the individual, it is important that care of the voice has already started to be addressed during the preparation period. You will then feel secure in the knowledge that your voice will be able to do justice to your material, having developed the stamina and flexibility needed.

> 'I was helped by concentrating on my breathing.'

There are books, tapes and videos available which will take you through the process of vocal development. These will include relaxation strategies, a consideration of the importance of posture, the practice of good breathing technique, the development of resonance and clarity to enable you to produce a clear, well-rounded voice, and the exploration of how the voice can make material interesting and memorable. A selection of these is listed at the end of this chapter. Training your voice takes time and commitment, and this makes it important to choose an approach that you feel comfortable with. Try to look at a range of these books to discover one which you find accessible and which advocates ideas you find compatible. As Bonnie Raphael (1997) comments in her paper *A consumer's guide to voice and speech training*, 'Ultimately, many of these seemingly diverse methods are in fact providing different doors into the same room.' Providing you stick at it, therefore, you are likely to achieve success whichever method you choose.

Communicating with your listeners

Visual aids again!

> 'A helpful strategy was to be well organised on the day.'

On the day of the presentation care should be taken to make sure that all visual aids are ready, in the right order and useable within the room allocated. Hardware such as OHPs, videos or tape-recorders should also be checked by you, both for defects and to ensure you are clear about how to use them. Taking time to complete these tasks can fulfil three needs. First, they ensure, as far as is possible, that your presentation will run smoothly. Second, having an opportunity to visit the space you will be using, you can make decisions with regard to the best place to position yourself and gain some feel for the acoustics. Third, they can go some way to combating your nerves, because having a job to do can divert your attention from worrying about what is to come.

During the presentation, bear in mind that this will be the first time the audience has seen any of your aids. They may need some time to take in the information. You can help them by directing their attention, ensuring they focus on appropriate elements: for example, by the use of a masking sheet and pointer in the case of an OHP acetate or by the use of gesture to draw the eye to artefacts. In any case, beware of removing the material too quickly; you might try out an appropriate speed on a friend or relation beforehand. A final point to remember is that you have come to talk to your listeners, not the visual aid! Make sure that your audience gets a fair share of your eye contact and body alignment – in other words, face them and not the aid.

Non-verbal communication

> 'I found it most helpful to make eye-contact and attempt to speak as I would normally speak in a group situation.'

When others can see us we begin to communicate with them, whether we verbalise or not. We do this through our use of non-verbal communication (NVC). We 'speak' with many other things besides the words we use: for example, through our body language, our facial expression, our clothes and our use of space. This is by no means a definitive list, but the common factor in these and other non-verbal channels is the ability of the audience to obtain its information from sources other than words. Argyle (1988: 5) points out that NVC has several different functions: it is used to express emotions, to communicate interpersonal attitudes, to accompany and support speech, to 'present the self' and as a part of many rituals. We can see that all of these functions come into play in making a presentation, whether formal or informal.

When you stand to make a presentation, you are inevitably going to be expressing emotion of some kind. The important thing is that the emotion you signal is one that has a positive rather than a negative effect on the listeners. You want your audience to feel sure that you will be able to deliver successfully. The audience wants to be able to relax and listen, but if they see another human being sending out lots of distress signals they begin to feel distressed too, aware that it is their presence that is causing the problem. Just think back to times when you have been made aware that someone is experiencing real difficulties – what were your feelings? Probably a mixture of concern for the individual and a desire to get away from the situation, because it made you uncomfortable. As a listener you want the speaker to make you feel relaxed and secure, not on tenterhooks. When it is you standing in front of your audience, it means that you may have to avoid showing how you really feel. If you have prepared well you should have confidence in your material; nevertheless, you may well be experiencing butterflies in the stomach, wobbly legs or other physical symptoms of nerves. You need to remind yourself that the vast majority of all speakers feel this way prior to a speech; it is a natural reaction. The important job you have to do is make sure that you are the only person who is aware of how you feel. This may seem an unfamiliar and Herculean task; however, it is something which most of us do at some points in our lives. For example, we may attempt to disguise how we feel when we visit relatives or go for an interview or find ourselves walking alone at night. In all these situations we may attempt to send out non-verbal signals that belie how we really feel inside, and giving a presentation is another of these.

Audiences are alert to your attitude. Subconsciously they ask themselves: does this person look as though they want to be here talking to us? Are they enthusiastic about their subject? Do they want to share their enthusiasm with us? For your presentation to go well it would be helpful if the answer to all these questions was 'yes'. Starting by smiling at your audience can go a good way towards ensuring that this will be the case. Atmosphere, while not visible, can still be felt, and listeners will perceive your smile as a signal that you are pleased to be there and that you want to interact with them. This will make them feel good, and they are likely to relax a little. This in turn will cause the atmosphere within the room to become more relaxed, something you will notice and feel good about. You are then more likely to send out further positive NVC and the process of you and your audience 'warming' to each other has begun.

Eye contact

> 'I think I would be most helped by having something visual to refer to, to take eyes away from me.'

On the whole, handbooks which offer strategies for managing public speaking give comprehensive and sound advice. They will all spend some time on eye contact, a powerful means of drawing your listeners in and making them feel that you are interested in them and want to interact with them. Many, however, make no mention of the effect of audience eye contact on you, the speaker. Anyone who has stood for the first time in front of an audience and looked out at the faces waiting expectantly will recognise the slightly unnerving experience of seeing so many pairs of eyes all focused on them. Unless we are in a relatively intimate relationship, we do not usually gaze so fixedly and for so long at others unless we are threatening them. You can see that being on the receiving end of all these 'stares' can seem worrying, and if you haven't been forewarned you could be triggered into the 'fight or flight' response, the usual human reaction to threat. Most of us will not take the fight option or run from the room; however, we can find ourselves producing what might be termed the 'ostrich effect'. We don't actually bury our heads in the sand, but we do withdraw eye contact from the object of our fear – we can't see them and so it doesn't feel quite so bad. We look at the floor or the ceiling or out of the window, anywhere where those eyes will not get to us, and then we feel better. Meanwhile, the poor audience is now confronted by someone who appears either totally terrified or so uninterested in them as an audience that they have switched off or are completely fascinated by something going on outside that they, the audience, can't see – all messages a speaker would want to avoid. Giving your listeners good eye contact tells them you are interested in them and that you want to talk to them. Withholding it does the opposite, so be brave and look at them.

Clothes

Clothing is another avenue of communication with your listener. There is evidence to show that people are responsive to those with similar appearance to themselves (Argyle 1988). On many occasions, if not most, you will be talking to groups with whom you share a common understanding. You are already a member of the education community and so are likely to have a good idea of the norms which prevail, allowing you to make informed decisions about your own dress code.

Dress can also make a difference to your performance. You need to be comfortable and confident in what you wear. Clothes that allow you to be you, that can be put on and forgotten, are perhaps the best. It is probably as well to give the newest addition to your wardrobe a miss if it has not been worn-in and any idiosyncrasies noted. Trailing sleeves that snag on equipment or buttons that refuse to say done up are the kinds of things that can catch you unawares and prove very distracting to you and your audience.

One other point: where possible, it pays to give some thought to the background against which you will be standing; you don't want to disappear into it, but on the other hand neither do you want to clash horribly.

Positioning and use of space

Where you position yourself will make a difference to how your audience perceives you. Try to avoid getting trapped behind pieces of equipment that obscure their view of you. If they have difficulty seeing you it will be harder to keep their attention.

When you look at the space beforehand, remember to have a look at the presenting area from the audience's point of view. Note spots where some of the audience will have problems seeing you. You need to remember to avoid these spots when you speak, or at least limit the time you spend there.

If you have any control over where you stand, for example in an informal context, make sure you do not stand in front of a source of light such as a window. If you do it will throw your face into shadow and the audience will be deprived of one of their main sources of information, your facial expression.

Remember that it will help to give you authority if you remain in one place for a length of time rather than wandering around or pacing up and down. However, moving at strategic times can be a useful means of providing an element of variety, the importance of which was discussed earlier.

How the listeners are positioned will also make a big difference to their experience. The greater the number of heads they have to look over, the less involved they are likely to be. One of the reasons I always try to visit a room before I use it is to make sure that the listeners get as clear a picture of me and I of them as is possible.

Using your voice to catch and maintain interest

> 'I'm worried about the audience getting bored and falling asleep.'

While this is a worry for lots of people, many of us don't really know how to go about preventing it, or what kind of things produce inattention in our listeners. This section highlights the skills we already possess which catch and maintain audience attention and which we need to consciously harness in order to enhance our presentation skills. It also points out some of those vocal traps we can fall into if we are unaware of potential problems.

Emphasis

In order to convey meaning and maintain our listeners' interest, we all possess a vital skill that we use in our everyday lives. When we speak we use a variety of ways to signal to the listener what is most important in what we are saying, and what least. If we did not do this our speech would sound robot-like, not human at all, and our listeners would have to work much harder to understand us.

In exercising this skill we emphasise the important phrases and words and 'throw away' those that are not so important. Take, for example, the sentence:

> 'When we compare the education system today with that of a hundred years ago we see many differences but also some worrying similarities.'

If we begin to break this sentence down we might feel that the most important words and phrases are 'compare', 'education system today', 'hundred years ago', 'many differences' and 'worrying similarities'. We have pulled out eleven words from a possible twenty-three. In other words, we have deemed half the sentence to be more important than the other half, and it is this important half we will emphasise. To do this we use any one or more of the following: we stretch out or elongate the words, taking longer over saying them; we pause before and/or after them; we say them at a different volume, either louder or sometimes quieter than the rest of the sentence; we use different intonation patterns on them; and we use tone of voice to convey our attitude to the ideas they are putting forward. At the same time we tend to speed up our delivery of the other words in the sentence, giving them less prominence. In this example sentence, I have made a rather crude division of words for the sake of simplicity. In reality there will be a subtle gradation in the emphasis we use, but the basic process is the same. Of course, for most of the time this goes on at a subconscious level. We know what we want to say and because of this we automatically give varying amounts of emphasis to our words. Problems can arise, however, when this natural process is interrupted by something like nervousness.

Pace and pause

When we are nervous we can find ourselves resorting to a range of unhelpful vocal behaviours. For example, some of us rush through our presentation in order to get it over with. This may make us feel better in the short term, but we certainly won't have done justice to the material we probably spent long hours preparing, and our listeners will have been short-changed. Because we have stopped using our usual emphasising techniques of taking longer over important words and using pauses to highlight them, the audience will have to work hard to follow our line of thought. If this state of affairs persists for more than a few minutes the listeners are likely to lose track altogether. Bombarded with information and with no time to take in one idea before they are hit by the next, they are likely to take refuge from the discomfort by switching off altogether.

On the other hand, there are some of us in whom nervousness produces the exact opposite of racing speech. For these people, delivery becomes a tortuously slow process. Their speech is full of irrelevant pauses which, to begin with, the listener interprets as signalling an important word or phrase. When none materialises they feel puzzled and then perhaps frustrated, eventually probably losing heart and switching off, as in the case of speech that is too fast.

In both cases, trying out your talk on a critical friend can be a helpful way of getting an idea of whether you need to adjust your speed.

Pitch

Another thing to watch out for is tension, caused by your nerves, sending the pitch of your voice sky high, giving it a squeaky quality. Women are more prone to this phenomenon as, generally, their natural vocal pitch is higher than men's and therefore reaches the 'squeaky zone' more quickly. A continuously high-pitched voice can be unpleasant to listen to and in addition, within our culture, is interpreted as lacking in authority.

On the other hand, there are some people who through nerves find themselves using only a restricted range of their lower pitches, and this tends to affect men more than women. These speakers are prone to sounding flat and dull.

Ensuring you keep your nerves under control is one avenue of attack on these problems. In addition, spending some preparation time experimenting with the pitch of your voice will allow you to manage it more successfully in stressful situations. Try speaking rhymes, prose or anything else at different pitches, thus becoming aware of the range you have and even extending it.

Tone

Nervousness can cause us to restrict or even shut down some of our usual channels of communication. When we are nervous we tend to be more physically restrained: for example, if waiting for an interview we are likely to sit tidily, not sprawled across the furniture as we might when relaxed at home. When under pressure we can also find ourselves becoming vocally restricted, resulting in a rather low-key and careful delivery. For most of us this is not a major problem, but for some, those who are normally fairly restrained in their everyday communication, it can mean becoming so low key they sound bored and indifferent. In this case, consciously trying to exaggerate or 'go over the top', as it is sometimes called, can be a means of bringing delivery to a level of animation which the listener will find comfortable and interesting.

Conclusion

If you have done your preparation well and practised, you will have laid firm foundations for a successful oral presentation. There is just one final element which needs to be included, and that is energy. Energy will help give your work an immediacy that will engage your listener. It will drive your talk forward, conveying enthusiasm and vitality; contagious qualities your listeners will pick up and respond to. Without energy a presentation can be a very pedestrian affair, but with it, it can prove an exhilarating experience for both audience and speaker. As some students commented at the end of their presentations, 'it went surprisingly well' and 'I was surprised at how much I enjoyed this part of the assignment'.

References

General

Argyle, M. (1988) *Bodily Communication*, second edition, London: Methuen.

Feltz, D.L. and Landers, D.M. (1983) 'The effects of mental practice on motor skill learning and performance: a meta-analysis', *Journal of Sport Psychology* 5: 25–57, cited in G.D. Wilson (1994) *Psychology for Performing Artists: Butterflies and Bouquets*, London: Jessica Kingsley Publications, 201.

Goleman, D. (1996) *Emotional Intelligence*, London: Bloomsbury.

Hayes, N. (1994) *Foundations of Psychology*, London: Routledge.

Nicholls, A. (1991) *How to Master Public Speaking*, Plymouth: How To Books.

Raphael, B.N. (1997) 'A consumer's guide to voice and speech training', in M. Hampton and B. Acker (eds) *The Vocal Vision: Views on Voice*, New York: Applause.

Robson, C. (1993) *Real World Research*, Oxford: Blackwell.

Suter, S. (1986) *Health Psychophysiology: Mind–Body Interactions in Wellness and Illness*, Hillsdale, NJ: Erlbaum Associates, cited in G.D. Wilson (1994) *Psychology for Performing Artists: Butterflies and Bouquets*, London: Jessica Kingsley Publications, 201.

Turk, C. (1985) *Effective Speaking: Communicating in Speech*, London: E. and F.N. Spon.

Voice

Berry, C. (1973/1994) *Voice and the Actor*, London: Harrap (1973), Virgin (1994).

Berry, C. (1975/1994) *Your Voice and How to Use it Successfully*, London : Harrap (1975), Virgin (1994).

Donaldson, E.L. (ed.) (1995) *Caring for Your Voice: Teachers and Coaches*, Calgary, Alberta: Detselig Enterprises.

Linklater, K. (1976) *Freeing the Natural Voice*, New York: Drama Book Specialists.

McCallion, M. (1988) *The Voice Book*, London: Faber and Faber.

Martin, S. and Darnley, L. (1996) *The Teaching Voice*, London: Whurr Publishers.

Morrison, M. (1977) *Clear Speech*, London: A. and C. Black.

Rodenburg, P. (1992) *The Right to Speak*, London: Methuen.

Coping with nerves

Bourne, E. (1995) *The Anxiety and Phobia Workbook*, second edition, Oakland: New Harbinger Publications.

Lloyd-Elliot, M. (1991) 'Witches, demons and devils: the enemies of auditions and how performing artists make friends with these saboteurs', in G.D. Wilson (ed.), *Psychology and Performing Arts*, Amsterdam: Swets and Zeitlinger.

Madders, J. (1979) *Stress and Relaxation*, London: Martin Dunitz.

Roland, D. (1997) *The Confident Performer*, Australia: Currency Press, London: Nick Hern Books.

Seligman, M.E.P. (1989) *Learned Optimism*, New York: Knopf.

Wilson, G.D. (1994) *Psychology for Performing Artists; Butterflies and Bouquets*, London: Jessica Kingsley Publications.

APPENDIX 8.1

Oral presentation

Thank you for your help in completing this questionnaire

1 Which of the following statements most closely mirrors your feelings about giving your oral presentation? (please tick your preferred response).
   (a) I feel confident about it.
   (b) Although the idea makes me nervous I think I will manage it.
   (c) I find the idea frightening and am afraid I will make a mess of it.
   (d) I know I won't be able to do it.

Comments:

2 In preparing for the oral presentation I think I would find the following helpful (please tick all that apply and number in order of preference with 1 as most preferred option).
   (a) Discussion with the rest of my group.
   (b) Discussion with others outside my group.
   (c) Writing my talk out.
   (d) Thinking about it on my own.
   (e) Practising aloud on my own.
   (f) Practising with the rest of my group.
   (g) Having a lecture on 'making an oral presentation'.

(h) Taking part in a workshop on 'making an oral presentation'.
(i) Other (please specify).

Comments:

3 For me, the most worrying aspect of giving an oral presentation is (please specify).

4 On the day I think I would be most helped by (please note down anything you or others might do that would help you).

APPENDIX 8.2

Year 2 Professional Studies – post-assignment feedback

Name (if you would prefer to remain anonymous, please leave blank):

Display and presentation day

Please comment on what you found the most helpful strategies for preparing for and managing this day with regard to your:

display

presentation

Professional Studies course

In retrospect please comment constructively on this course.

9 Starting your research project

Rosalyn George

The context

The aims and purposes of this chapter are to examine the 'process of research' in the context of education. I will explore the nature and purposes of educational research, and the contemporary debates surrounding what are and what are not appropriate methods and approaches, alongside a brief examination of the logistics and practicalities of undertaking a research project. In the space available this chapter cannot provide a guide to every research method, nor can it cover statistical analyses. However, there is currently a wealth of literature which deals with step-by-step approaches to research methods, and references to useful texts will be made throughout.

Teaching as a profession is currently undergoing a substantial restructuring process. The 1994 Education Act gave rise to the creation of an agency that is charged with the responsibility of managing the teaching workforce from the point of entry of a student teacher undertaking their education and training, be it undergraduate or postgraduate, to beginner teacher, then expert or subject specialist teacher, through to middle and senior manager and eventually to headship. The National Professional Standards and Qualifications (NPSQ) framework that is now in place will identify, for every stage of an individual's career, a clear set of standards or benchmarks that will define their 'fitness for purpose'. These standards, however, tend to define the process of teaching as though it is an uncontested, technical procedure. In this new climate, therefore, it becomes imperative that student teachers and qualified teachers – be they at the beginning of their career or experienced individuals – do not consider the role of research as something apart from their day-to-day existence, but instead engage in research as an integral part of their role as 'professionals': for example, the curriculum needs to be viewed as something organic that is continuously subject to influence and change, and teachers as reflective practitioners need to be part of this development process.

What do we understand by educational research?

Today, research is no longer confined to the laboratory but is undertaken by many people in a variety of settings. It is essentially a social activity carried out in a methodical way to inform and develop thinking and reflection, of either an individual action or a group's collaborative ventures. There are many different kinds of research but the common characteristic of all these approaches is that 'research is a systematic process by which we know more about something than we did before engaging in the process' (Merrian and Simpson 1984: iv). The systematic inquiry can, however, when dealing with people and events outside the laboratory (which allows a deal of control), be a 'complex, relatively poorly controlled and generally messy' situation (Robson 1993: 6). Nevertheless, all educational research which is carefully planned and is systematically carried out is aimed at deepening our understanding of the role, purpose and function of education in and for society.

Within the research community there are intense debates about, for example, what are and what are not the most appropriate methods to employ, especially concerning the appropriateness of 'qualitative' or 'quantitative' approaches. Qualitative approaches and quantitative approaches to research have been simplistically viewed as ideologically and methodologically at odds with each other.

Qualitative research is concerned with understanding people and how they view the world, and it is about research with people rather than on people (Reason 1994). Qualitative research asserts that inquiry cannot be value-free – indeed it is value-bound by the choice of research, the analysis of the data, the values of those doing the investigation and those being investigated (Biondo 1998). Qualitative researchers see research as an activity in which the researched and the researcher participate and work collaboratively. An ethnographic model of research, for example, adopts a qualitative approach. The ethnographer establishes a many-sided and often long-term relationship with a community in its own naturalistic setting. Such interactive and dynamic relationships 'exclude the preconceptions that researchers have and expose them to a new social milieu which demands their engagement' (May 1997). Hence, the context in which the interactions happen is viewed as a critical part of the research process.

Quantitative research, however, is a more traditional approach and presents the view that research is concerned with establishing natural and universal laws which regulate and determine individual and social behaviour. This approach is concerned with discovering general laws, and regards the social world as orderly, adhering to the rules of the natural world. This 'scientific' approach sees research as analysing discrete and distinct areas in a detached and objective way. Quantitative researchers, for example, tend to use large-scale surveys in their research and by asking the same question in the same way to a very large sample of people they feel able to generalise and present their findings as being representative of the population at large. 'Quantitative researchers collect facts and study the relationship of one set of facts to another. They measure, using scientific techniques that are likely to produce quantified and, if possible, generalisable conclusions' (Bell 1993: 5).

While researchers are usually orientated one way or another, most adopt a mix of both these approaches to explore and investigate a social world that is dynamic and changing. The distinction between qualitative and quantitative research is mainly relevant at the level of methods and it can have implications at the level of theory. The two approaches can be summarised as follows:

Qualitative

- The researcher gets close to the source of the data.
- The researcher can adopt an insider's perspective.
- The researcher is engaged in a more fluid approach that acknowledges the reality that not all variables can be tightly controlled.
- The researcher can adopt a 'participant observer' model of collecting data.
- The researcher can use semi-structured or unstructured interviews on a one-to-one or group basis, where the interviewer elicits data as they listen to the interactions.

Quantitative

- The researcher seeks facts or causes of social phenomenon.
- The researcher takes no account of social meaning.
- The researcher stays at arm's length from the data source.
- The researcher adopts an outsider perspective which assumes that this detached form of engagement provides a considerable degree of objectivity.
- The research is outcome focused.
- There is controlled measurement through the use of questionnaires, structured interviews, surveys and check lists.

The nature of doing small-scale, classroom-based research which is practitioner-led lends itself naturally towards qualitative approaches. This chapter identifies itself with this approach and will refrain from examining the quantitative aspects since this would entail the acquisition of a set of statistical skills and understandings before one can confidently engage in such a paradigm. Professional researchers need these skills and understandings. For a basic level of familiarity with quantitative research techniques, the following reading will be useful: Radical Statistics

Education Group (1982) *Reading Between The Numbers: A Critical Guide to Educational Research*, London: BSSRS Publications.

Doing research

As researchers, we bring to the research process our histories, our experiences and our stories. The choice of our research focus should be something that drives us and that we have a need and a desire to know more about. The values and views of the researcher, in terms of where they are coming from and in many ways whose side they are on, cannot be discounted. It is not a neutral activity. The researcher needs to be aware of the many shared understandings that they may have with the 'subject' (people and the community being researched), and should therefore be able to interrogate the data and the emerging trends that arise out of the data critically to ensure that the conclusions drawn are both robust and valid (see section on 'Analysis and interpretation of the data'). Cultural assumptions – who we are, what we know and where we come from – directly affect the research process in terms of planning, design, writing and subsequent interpretations. This raises the question about whether the cultural, political and social background of the researcher might constitute a 'problem' in the research process. This is an important consideration because the researcher and the researched may come from different backgrounds, both socially and culturally. Hence, their interpretations are liable to be different. The research community's goals can often conflict with those that are being researched. What is crucial is to be aware that the research is as important to others as it is to yourself. How far do researchers need to be grounded as an actual person in a concrete setting (Stanley 1990: 12) with their study before they proceed – can a researcher from the dominant group study the experiences of subordinated groups? In the context of social policy, for example:

> feminists argue that the androcentric [male] values of male researchers affect all aspects of their research practice from design, through data collection to interpretation and application ... social researchers may be heterosexist in their methods and interpretation believing and perpetuating, for example, that a 'normal' and 'legitimate' family is one man and one woman who are married with children.
>
> (May 1997: 48)

It goes without saying that the technical skills required for research – for example data handling, interpretation and writing – can be acquired through experience, but to critically engage in and understand the research possibly requires an ability to de-centre. Reflexivity (to reflect upon why an action is taken), it would seem, needs to be a critical part of the research process. Despite these caveats, the many 'successful' studies undertaken suggest that reflexivity has not been a necessary prerequisite. Nevertheless, a shared experience will give the researcher a better understanding of the implications, not only in the choice of subject but how data is generated and how significance is evaluated (Scott and Usher 1996: 36).

Identifying your research question

The first stage in undertaking research is the choosing of the research question and reflecting upon the reasons for that choice. Choosing a professional or personal issue that one feels passionately about can be important, because if one's interest flags, the whole process can become a chore. Furthermore, a study that is also of value to the participating communities in which their voices and needs are heard can be socially and morally important. Interestingly, in the current educational climate, which encourages teamwork in schools, plus the increasing influence of feminist collaborative approaches to writing and research, there is still a great deal of resistance by many practitioners to models of enquiry which are collaborative and co-operative (Seale 1995; see also Roberts 1990).

The researcher will need to get to know the broad context in which their study is to be situated, any past research in the chosen area and any academic literature in that field. This will equip and aid the researcher in the research design, and will inform the theoretical and methodological choices that can be considered. The importance of having a clear research question needs to be emphasised, because 'If research is not grounded in clear questions there is a danger that the results will be unclear or say nothing' (Light *et al.* 1990: 13). However, if research is considered as a dynamic and evolving process, then the question too will be part of the overall process and thus will enable the focus to move from the general to the specific. Bell (1993: 5–14) warns about the pitfalls of taking a rather too general approach to research, for such an approach can encourage researchers to gather vast amounts of very general data with the hope and expectation that some kind of pattern will emerge. The journey made towards identifying the research question will be eased, as well as being informed, if preliminary reading is undertaken in the general area of the research.

Reading for research

Reading is an integral part of the process of research. A literature review takes one on a tour of the range of existing material that is accessible and available. Furthermore, it provides the researcher, at an early stage, with a heightened sense of what is worth investigating and what is not. Research is cumulative and builds on the work of others. Reading locates us as researchers in a relationship to the literature in the field. By engaging with both past and contemporary work, it informs us about what has already been done in the area and what remains unresolved. Reading helps us to determine the level of theory and knowledge already in existence – is it explanatory, predictive, descriptive, etc.? It will give us a sense of the sort of methods other researchers have employed to undertake their research – how big or small were their samples, how reliable were they, etc.? In a weak dissertation the literature floats freely and does not relate specifically to the study. The literature should inform and underscore one's work even if it runs counter to the data, and should represent all sides of the debate. In addition, your literature review may need to take in the ever-increasing range and number of educational policy documents emanating from the DfEE and other government agencies.

A researcher needs to selectively read texts, and the ability to skim and speed read can be invaluable (see also Chapter 6). Reading summaries and reviews can be extremely useful and save time. However, it is important to remember that whenever a source of information is considered potentially useful, details of the source of that information should be noted and, more importantly, recorded in a systematic way.

Supervision as a collaborative venture

Researchers at undergraduate or postgraduate level often seem to view research as a semi-autonomous activity and, as such, tutorial support may not be as eagerly sought or considered easily accessible. However, a supervised research project should be regarded as a collaborative venture which can benefit both parties. A supervisor may have far less knowledge about the particular project being researched, but they will have experience of doing research themselves and will therefore be familiar with the process, the likely pitfalls and the attendant anxieties. The role of the supervisor is to assist the researcher in reflecting upon their work. 'Reflection requires a mirror. Tutors are the "Others" who provide such mirrors' (Seale 1995). The researcher will need to plan their tutorials and, before meeting with their supervisor, will benefit from the tutorial if they have already submitted a draft of some of their work to focus the discussions – otherwise the tutorial may drift without anything concrete arising from the interaction. Taking a list of questions to the tutorials can also help to make the most of the time allocated. Keeping in touch with your supervisor on a regular basis throughout the process and using them as a sounding board can also be invaluable. Do not wait until you have a more or less complete draft before arranging an appointment, not only because this could result in the tutorial time becoming crowded with information, but also because less feedback, a little and often, is more effective.

At the end of the tutorial, be sure that what is expected by the next scheduled tutorial is agreed. Remember that getting the most from tutorials requires careful planning and much effort on the part of the researcher. If there is a failure to submit a draft, it is unlikely that the supervisor will chase you for it, and it may be seen, fairly or unfairly, as a lack of interest and concern on the researcher's part. Supervisors prefer researchers who are excited and interested in their work.

Students themselves following the same or similar courses can provide invaluable help for each other by setting up support networks. Such groups can raise the level of consciousness of the individual and as such enable the individual levels of effort and expertise to be shared (see also Chapter 2).

Conducting your research – approaches to adopt

Before settling on an approach to take, there are some pertinent issues that need to be considered at an early stage. First, if the research is to be conducted in an institution, for example a school or an 'off-site' unit, there are issues of access that have to be negotiated. The logistics involved have to be considered in terms of time needed for doing the fieldwork, the numbers of staff and pupils involved and the amount of disruption that this is likely to cause. Second, there are issues of ethics and confidentiality that also need to be negotiated and agreed upon. These are matters of fundamental importance and can impact upon every stage of the research. *Agreed Codes of Practice of the British Sociological Association and the British Psychological Association* should inform one's practice (see Robson 1993: 470–8 for details of these codes). Third, in a current climate of 'partnership' between any of the following: Higher Education Institutions (HEIs), schools and parents, it is important that researchers should make that partnership a very real one in practice. Issues of power relations that are inherent within the project should be made explicit and, wherever possible, the imbalances should be adjusted and corrected. In the context of pre-service teacher education, the shared responsibilities for the education and training of future teachers between HEIs and schools means that any research that is carried out in a school or a similar institution takes account of the triangulation involved: that is, the collection of data from a number of sources and informants and comparing and contrasting the different accounts in order to ascertain as full and balanced a picture as possible. Teacher mentors and professional tutors and pupils in school should be closely involved in the research, and thus contribute to the pool of 'collective intelligence' that informs both theory and practice.

As outlined earlier in this chapter, you have to decide and settle on an approach or a mix of approaches to adopt in conducting research. The approach you adopt will depend on the question or hypothesis that you frame, which in turn will have emerged from your initial reading in the area and from discussions with peers, tutors and your supervisor. The tentative question and/or hypothesis will then lead on to planning the project and developing a research proposal. The research proposal should be seen as indicative rather than binding. Developing a research proposal ensures that you will think deeply about the questions you wish to investigate, and this can help enormously in focusing your topic at the outset.

Selecting methods of data collection

Access to sources of data requires careful thought and detailed scheduling. Once these are settled, one can then move on to examining ways of collecting data for the project. This may be done through interviews, questionnaires, keeping of diaries/journals, school policy documents or observations. You need to keep reminding yourself of your research question, and asking whether the method you adopt is the most suitable one for generating the data you need. You need to also consider time constraints, cost (typing, travel, etc.) and access to informants (i.e. individuals and members of the community you wish to interview). What follows is an overview of the most popular research methods which have been developed and used by practitioners in the educational field.

Interviewing

By far the most popular method of data collection for teacher and student researchers is through interviewing. The interview can be a rewarding method of obtaining in-depth qualitative data. It is popular because it probably appears at first sight to be unproblematic and easy to administer – after all, we all talk all of the time. With teacher-led research, the informants are often real experts in the shape of schoolchildren, and as such you have to ensure that you do not impose your agenda on them and that you keep them talking freely and openly with the minimum amount of intervention. This intervention may take the form of nodding or following up interesting responses or underlying motives. Non-verbal responses can also provide further information for understanding the verbal response. Because the interview is a flexible method for finding out, considerable skill is called for on the part of the interviewer, who needs to be mindful of the potential for bias within the process; for example, interviewers may affect an interviewee's reply simply by the manner in which they ask the question. As every word or pause in an interview counts, you will need to record the whole process accurately, preferably with an audio tape-recorder, and then transcribe the interview later. You may need to pilot the interview to test the suitability of the questions – do they provide you with the kind of information you want? You may wish to run the interview in order to time it and to allow you to familiarise yourself with the schedule, to produce a natural and relaxed setting when undertaking the interview proper.

There tend to be three types of interview. The first is the 'structured' interview. This is rather like a questionnaire where there is a predetermined set of questions on a standardised schedule: each person is asked the same question in the same way so that any differences in answers are deemed to be real ones and not the result of the interview process. The interviewer fills in a response sheet as the interview proceeds. This type of interviewing procedure is associated with large-scale surveys, such as telephone surveys, and adopts a quantitative approach. May (1997) observes that 'structured' interview success depends on the interviewer being similar to the target group, who in turn need to understand the culture of the interviewer in order that the interpretation of the questions and the dynamics of the interview do not vary to any significant extent.

The 'semi-structured' interview is where the interviewer has worked out a set of questions in advance which can be modified depending on the interviewee's response. In this model, questions can be omitted or added depending on what is revealed within the interview; the interviewer is also able to probe behind the responses. This model of interviewing enables the respondent to answer more in their own terms. It is important for the interviewer, therefore, to understand that the context of the interview is an important aspect of the process. Within an educational setting, often this type of interview is the most favoured, for, as stated above, the real experts may be schoolchildren who need to be able to talk freely within a 'semi-structured' setting.

Lastly, the 'unstructured' interview is a model where the interviewer has a general area of interest and allows the conversation around the topic to flow freely and develop. The interviewer has an aim in mind, but the interviewee is able to employ their own frames of reference. The method of interviewing is located very clearly in the qualitative approach of researching. Many feminist researchers use 'unstructured' and open-ended interviewing, on the basis that access is offered to people's ideas, thoughts and memories in their own words rather than in the words of the researcher. This is particularly important with regard to the study of women, in that learning from women is an antidote to a history of women's ideas being ignored, or having men speak for women (Reinharz 1992).

Questionnaires

The questionnaire is often viewed as 'clean' research where the researcher is able to distance themselves from the respondent. Questionnaires are located within a quantitative method of research and are often associated with large-scale surveys. Large-scale questionnaires are seen as a central part of social research, for they are able to rapidly and relatively inexpensively discover particular thinking or views of the population at large. Questionnaires are one of the most frequently used methods employed by government to collect data on a regular basis, and are characterised by the use of large or very large numbers, for example a hundred or several thousand people. Questionnaires are a good way of collecting certain kinds of information, assuming that there is a good response rate. A response rate of 40 per cent from a postal questionnaire is generally considered the acceptable rate, and you may even achieve a higher rate after sending out reminders. Questionnaires are efficient in terms of researchers' time and effort – for example, one could potentially get thirty or forty responses in the time it takes to do one interview – and their anonymity can be advantageous if dealing with sensitive issues (May 1997). Questionnaires tend to be reliable insofar as you can give the same questionnaire to different groups or the same group before and after an event and then compare the results, and if they are well constructed they are easier to analyse. Computer-aided programs can also be used.

However, as with any method adopted, you will need to reflect on the questionnaire's suitability for generating the data you wish to gather. Designing a good questionnaire is a difficult task: questions need to be kept simple and straightforward, for the researcher is in no position to know how the question has been interpreted by the respondent, and there is no possibility of probing beyond the answer. You cannot be sure how respondents make sense of your questions, and while you can use 'open-ended' questions, these take longer to analyse. Questionnaires also tend to set the agenda and make it difficult to discover what people really think or what is important to them. With classroom-based research, which tends to be small-scale, questionnaires may not always be the best approach to adopt. (See Oppenheim 1966.)

The following points may be useful to consider when constructing a questionnaire.

- Avoid ambiguous or imprecise questions.
- Do not assume any specialist knowledge which respondent may not have.
- Do not ask respondents to recall events that happened some time ago.
- Avoid asking a question within a question (these are known as triple headers). It is better to ask three separate questions.
- Avoid leading questions, hypothetical questions or insensitive questions.
- All questionnaires should be typed up and well spaced.
- Give clear instructions: for instance, if you are using an attitude scale provide an example at the beginning indicating the weightings on the scale.
- Avoid 'open questions' because they give greater rise to differences in interpretation.
- Consider the cost of sending out the questionnaire and the cost of returning it.

- Ensure that you have access to relevant equipment for analysing responses, etc.

Observation

'As the actions and behaviour of people are a central aspect in virtually any inquiry, a natural and obvious technique is to watch, and then to describe, analyse and interpret what we have observed' (Robson 1993: 190). Observation is an excellent way of gathering data directly rather than relying on what people may report as happening. (See Bateman and Gottman 1986; Hurst 1991.) When carrying out an observation, the aim is to take in information and not to respond to it. This is a difficult task with children, as they certainly want to involve you in their activities. As with all research approaches, the research question will determine the strategy for observational work. There tend to be two main strategies, one being 'participant observation', the second 'structured observation'.

Participant observation involves a rather naturalistic method where the observer keeps a running record of events, activities and interventions of the individual or group, and is largely unstructured. In 'early years' work, this method often targets an individual child (Sylva *et al.* 1980), and then combines this use of a qualitative approach with a coding system, a quantitative approach. (A coding system is a set of predetermined categories for recording what is observed.) The problem with such an approach is that it generates masses of data and therefore analysing the content can be very time-consuming.

Structured observation involves:

- time sampling – this ascertains frequency patterns of behaviour, for example how often a child claims teacher attention;
- event sampling – this concentrates on a particular short period of behaviour;
- checklists – these are used for recording stages of development, best thought of as summaries of observations. Checklists include rating scales, for example 'keen to work' to 'never works'. The disadvantages of using such a checklist is that you limit your record of what is going on.

Diaries and journals

It is important for you to keep your own diary or journal throughout the research process as a way of recording your thoughts and ideas as they develop. They will provide a place to record all the bits and pieces of information as they arrive until you have time to properly assess their worth (Seale 1995). You can record critical incidents in your journal and provide a developing picture of your work in progress. It should be a great aide-memoir when you come to writing up your project.

Research diaries for your respondents are an attractive way of generating data, for they appear on the surface to require minimum effort by the researcher for maximum output by the respondent. Diaries, however, can lead to accusations of bias. Robson (1993) cites an example of some university lecturers who were asked to keep a diary which reflected their weekly workload. The diaries suggested that the lecturers' hours were immense. However, the respondents' knowledge that the diaries were to be used for a pay claim led to issues relating to objectivity. It is therefore important that you agree a way of keeping the diary with the respondent; they need to know what they have to do, why and when – for example, an end-of-day commentary or a running commentary over a specific period of time, etc.

Documents

The use of documents in the research process allows comparisons to be made against the researcher's interpretation of events and those recorded in documents. They can tell us a great deal about the way events were constructed at the time and about the intentions and aspirations of the period of time to which they refer. Use of primary source documentation, such as school prospectuses, minutes from meetings, information leaflets, children's work, letters to parents, newspapers and magazines, etc., will provide you with further material to supplement data gathered from other sources and, because of their permanence, may result in few problems at a practical level regarding 'content analysis'. Content analysis is the term given to the process of examining evidence in detail and identifying themes, patterns of beliefs or behaviour (Edwards 1990).

Analysis and interpretation of data

Qualitative research can generate mountains of data. Managing this data effectively and analysing it can be a major issue. The data may consist of primary source documentation, such as school prospectuses or any other public documents, fieldwork notes and observations, simple diary accounts and reflections in the field, and transcribed interviews. There is first a need to attempt to reduce the size and scope of this data. There are common techniques for coding data and methods of classifying groups; Robson (1993: Part 4) provides a comprehensive guide to these techniques. Second, emerging themes need to be grouped and laid out clearly so that they are manageable. This means looking for differences, similarities, patterns and anything of significance. The data can be annotated and it is important not to categorise it prematurely. One should also look for significant absences, and for data that goes against the grain. Concepts can emerge from an imaginative analysis of the data, and from reading the mass of literature (hence the importance of linking the literature review with the data).

Writing up your research

It is important to write from the word go, even though much of the beginning writing may not find its way into the final dissertation or study. Your writing should represent the research process, providing accounts at various stages. For many people, starting to write is a hard task. Bell (1993) cites Bogdan and Biklen (1982), who maintain that novice writers are the big procrastinators and find a million and one reasons for not getting started. Robson (1993) suggests blocking out periods of productive time or leaving a session in mid-paragraph so that you can pick up the writing process more easily next time. Ely *et al.* (1997) take the view that research writing can be 'multifaceted' and 'multi informed' and can be composed of a number of literary traditions and devices. They identify a number of narrative terms, for example vignettes, layered stories, anecdotes, pastiches (literary quilt). For them, meaning is often constructed through story. The importance of having a clear sense of who your audience is will help in the writing-up stage: your report will be different if you were presenting it to a tabloid newspaper or as a PhD thesis. The presentation of the overall report needs to be structured, and this structure may be helpful to you when writing. In almost all cases, the institution examining and validating the report will give very clear guidelines on the way it should be structured. During the writing up of your dissertation you will need to cite and refer to a variety of texts and articles you have used and consulted during your research. You should systematically record all these references as you progress through your project. This information is crucial and will save you days of library searching when writing up your work (Box 9.1 provides a useful guide to recording references).

Box 9.1 Recording references to information that you have read

A common and popular way to record references is to buy a card box file and a set of blank cards. Note the authors, title, place of publication and date of every book you read on these cards. If you are reading a chapter in an edited collection also note the chapter author, the title of the chapter and the page numbers of the chapter. For articles you will need author, title, journal, volume, page numbers and date (Edwards 1990). There are many different ways of referencing your material, but often the Harvard system is recommended (see Chapter 6).

Conclusion

Educational research in the UK is at the crossroads. The agencies responsible for education provision and standards in education have all entered the fray, arguing about whether current educational research is dealing sufficiently or adequately with the everyday issues and concerns of classroom teachers. This has led to considerable debate about the health of educational research in the United Kingdom. The issues raised in this chapter are intended to engage the beginner teacher and the experienced practitioner with the understandings and the desires to undertake research on classroom issues and everyday practice and, in the process, engage with the complexities of learning and teaching. It is vital that through practitioner-based research, teacher researchers will increasingly enter into the debate about the real relevance of theory-making and its direct contribution to classroom practice.

References

Bateman, R. and Gottman, J.M. (1986) *Observing Interaction*, Cambridge: Cambridge University Press.

Bell, J. (1993) *Doing Your Research Project*, Buckingham: Open University Press.

Biondo, D (1998) 'What sort of research in education do you consider of most value?', unpublished MA paper, Goldsmiths College, University of London.

Bogdan, R.C. and Biklen, S.K. (1982) *Qualitative Research for Education: An Introduction to Theory and Methods*, Boston, Mass.: Allyn and Bacon.

Edwards, A. (1990) *Practitioner Research; Study Guide No. 1*, Lancaster: St Martin's College.

Ely, M., Vinz, R., Downing, M. and Anzul, M. (1997) *On Writing Qualitative Research: Living by Words*, London: Falmer.

Hurst, V. (1991) *Planning for Early Years*, London: Paul Chapman.

Light, R., Singer, J. and Willett, J. (1990) *By Design: Planning Research On Higher Education*, London: Harvard University Press.

May, T. (1997) *Social Research; Issues, Methods and Processes*, Buckingham: Open University Press.

Merrian, S. and Simpson, E. (1984) *A Guide to Research for Educators and Trainers of Adults*, Florida: Krieger Publishing Company.

Oppenheim, A.N. (1966) *Questionnaire Design and Attitude Measurement*, London: Heinemann.

Reason, P. (ed.) (1994) *Participation in Human Inquiry*, London: Sage.

Reinharz, S. (1992) *Feminist Methods in Social Research*, New York: Oxford University Press.

Roberts, H. (ed.) (1990) *Doing Feminist Research*, London: Routledge, Chapter 2.

Robson, C. (1993) *Real World Research*, Oxford: Blackwell Publishers.

Scott, D. and Usher, R. (eds) (1996) *Understanding Educational Research*, London: Routledge.

Seale, G. (1995) *The Primary Education Dissertation. A Handbook for Students*, Chichester: Chichester Institute of Higher Education.

Stanley, L. (1990) *Feminist Praxis: Research, Theory and Epistemology in Feminist Sociology*, London: Routledge.
Sylva, K., Roy, C. and Painter, M. (1980) *Childwatching at Play Group and Nursery School*, London: Grant McIntyre.

10 Establishing and maintaining professional working relationships

Sue Kendall

Introduction

The relationships established during work in school with professional and support staff, parents and children greatly influence study at all levels within the world of education and have a significant impact upon the success and performance of all involved. Indeed, education degrees are one of the few professional qualifications where students are actually assessed on their ability to form and work within professional relationships.

This chapter draws upon original research data which was gathered from a range of people studying and working in education. Questionnaires were distributed to undergraduate and postgraduate students and those working towards their master's degree. It was anticipated that the issues facing the master's students might vary according to whether they were studying on a full-time or in-service course, and thus both groups were included in the sample. The questionnaire posed a range of open questions for reflection and response. Students were asked to comment on examples of positive and negative incidents they had experienced, particularly when working with adults in the school context. They were also asked to identify the key individuals with whom they needed to establish a working relationship. The composition of the questionnaire was informed by the experiences that I and my colleagues have of co-ordinating the placement of students in London schools and tutoring master's level students. As part of our quality assurance procedures we regularly collect feedback from all those involved in our partnership with schools, including students, teachers and tutors. Conclusions have also been drawn from analysis of this documentation.

There are a range of models of practice which operate when a student is working in a school, whether they are on their first school experience placement or involved in collecting data for a research project. Participants may be aware of the model(s) in use but very often those involved may have differing perceptions of their respective roles. Fish (1989) highlights this point with reference to the role of the class teacher in initial teacher education. She notes that in current practice an 'apprenticeship' model tends to be adopted, where the class teacher perceives their role as providing the opportunity for the student to learn from them. I would argue that the 'competency-based' curriculum, which education courses are currently required to provide, supports this model in that there is an assumed list of skills that the student can observe and practice.

The philosophy that underpins our work and the research for this chapter are grounded in a commitment to equality for all those involved in supporting students in school. The model operated is one which aims to develop reflective practitioners (Whitty 1995), and it is made explicit to all concerned that this includes listening to, and responding to, 'all voices involved' (Kendall *et al.* 1997).

It follows then that this chapter is organised to express a range of issues from a variety of perspectives. Table 10.1 sets out the key individuals identified by respondents as those who played a central role in their work in school, and provides a map for the chapter. This chapter is divided into two sections, each exploring the roles of – and issues of particular relevance for – first, those involved in undergraduate and postgraduate initial teacher training, and second, those involved in continuing professional development, School-Centred Initial Teacher Training or returning to further part- or full-time study. Each section also contains a discussion of the role of the student within the school context and explores particular strategies for establishing and maintaining positive working relationships. Having analysed the data it appeared that there was some overlap for those returning to study, in terms of key individuals and related issues. Table 10.1 identifies these with an asterisk, and they are discussed together in the text in the second section under 'Common issues and relationships'. Although the reader is directed to the section of particular interest, it is hoped that the issues raised will be of interest to a range of readers. The emphasis is on working relationships with adults in the school context.

The issues explored in this chapter are of relevance to those working in a variety of school settings from nursery through to subject departments in secondary schools. The term 'class teacher' is used in a generic sense to refer to teachers with whole class responsibility in the primary sector as well as those working within subject departments in the secondary phase. Similarly, the terms 'school-based tutor' and 'college-based tutor' are used to refer to the persons who have supervisory responsibility for the student, even though many university partnerships may choose to use alternative terms such as 'mentor' or 'supervisor'.

Table 10.1 The key individuals involved in forming professional working relationships in school

Course of study	*Key individuals*
Initial Teacher Training (ITT) BA(QTS) and PGCE.	Student Class teacher(s)/subject teacher(s) School-based tutor/mentor Supervising college tutor(s) Headteacher/senior manager Support staff Parents
Continuing Professional Development (CPD), those returning to part-time study and School-Centred Initial Teacher Training (SCITT).	Student Colleagues Headteacher/senior manager College tutor(s)* External agencies* Parents*
Those returning to full-time study	Student Class teachers/subject teachers Headteacher(s)/senior manager College tutor(s)* External agencies* Parents*

Note: *Those categories marked with an asterisk are discussed together under 'Common issues and relationships'.

Initial Teacher Training (ITT)

The role of the student

Those students who choose to embark upon a course of initial teacher training come to the profession for a range of reasons, having had very different life experiences. Similarly each student will have a unique perception of education, this having been informed by a range of factors including their own experiences of schooling. All of these factors combine to significantly affect their ability to establish and maintain professional working relationships once they are in schools.

For some students beginning an undergraduate course, it will be the first time they have been in a professional working environment, although many will have had, or be working in, some form of paid employment to support their studies. For those who are entering college or university straight from their own schooling, there is a shift of perception to be made. They are no longer the receiving pupil, but now have to take on the responsibilities associated with providing learning opportunities and work alongside teachers as colleagues. Those students entering the postgraduate courses will have already experienced academic success with their first degree, but can sometimes be surprised by the pace and intensity of their education course.

Many students enter full-time study after a period of work, and for some this will mean making the transition from being qualified in their field to a position where they are now the learner. If the career change is quite radical there is often a 'culture shock' associated with being in a totally different working environment. One student, who moved from being a bank clerk, commented that she found the flexibility, reflection and analysis required by her course extremely challenging, yet very rewarding.

A substantial number of mature students following undergraduate and postgraduate courses have made the decision to pursue a career in teaching after they have supported their own children's learning, either at home or as a parent assistant in school. Many hold strong views about the practice they have observed as their children have been taught. As with those who have moved into teaching having been nursery nurses or classroom assistants, it is important that these students are open to the breadth of new ideas their course will introduce.

It appears essential that the student is able to develop and be confident in their role if they are to be able to establish positive working relationships with adults around them in school. Fish (1989) cites a range of examples of confusion over roles and responsibilities and how this can lead to the development of a negative or confused working relationship. A crucial factor lies in balancing the needs for personal development against those of the school and the children's learning. As part of this, it is essential that the student is confident in their interpretation of both school and college expectations, and where there are potential conflicts negotiate between the class teacher, school and college-based tutors. Sensitivity and flexibility are required, whether it is in adopting a particular dress code or negotiating responsibility for units of work. An analysis of quality assurance questionnaires and informal discussions with teachers reveals that they consider it important that the students are prepared to be committed (i.e. putting in the hours), to act upon advice given and to take some initiative.

One important aspect of the role of the student is that in all relationships they assume a responsibility for trying to make them as positive as possible. Thus they may have to seek advice, initiate conversations, ask questions, make their needs known, and, if difficulties arise, seek advice from others involved, such as the headteacher, tutors at college or colleagues.

The role of the class teacher

Above all, the teacher is responsible for the day-to-day learning that takes place. This requires involvement in long-, medium- and short-term planning and the consequent assessment and record-keeping of the children's progress. Many teachers also manage a number of qualified or volunteer helpers in the classroom. They are also responsible for liaising, both formally and informally, with other colleagues including the headteacher and parents. The majority of experienced class teachers also have responsibility for a curriculum area in a primary school, and within the secondary phase may be involved in the management of a department.

In terms of their relationship with a student, the role of the class teacher is focused upon those aspects of their work which relate primarily to the classroom. Responses from students and teachers working in the primary partnership have highlighted the following as areas where the student might expect to receive support from their class teacher. It is perhaps interesting to note that the list highlights the practical and explicit aspects of the class teacher's role and does not include, for example, reference to pastoral responsibilities. These areas are:

- planning;
- knowledge of curriculum areas;
- insights into and evaluations of individual children's learning;
- classroom management;
- assessment and record-keeping procedures;
- discipline strategies;
- liaison with colleagues and parents;
- display.

Class teachers can provide support and feedback on a student's practice in a number of ways, both formal and informal. They will usually be interested in the student's planning and paperwork, and may ask to look through files. Some teachers will provide written notes or verbal feedback about lessons they have observed. Often these will provide the student with constructive ideas and can form the basis of discussion and help for the student in setting targets for future development.

The class teacher's role in assessment will vary according to the supervision arrangements in place. If he or she is involved in making formal assessments, it would appear important that both parties identify the times when a student is being judged on their performance and when the teacher is involved in supporting a developing colleague. This has been highlighted by school-based colleagues working in the primary partnership. They suggest that, wherever possible, the student should not be placed in a position where their class teacher is also their tutor. Where this does arise it may prove necessary for the student to take the initiative and highlight the dual roles and, with their teacher, discuss how they are to manage them, if necessary calling upon the college-based tutor for advice.

Class teachers have increasing demands being placed upon them which often require time devoted to after-hours meetings and paperwork. The introduction of the National Curriculum saw the beginning of an ongoing process to review the curriculum. The past years have seen a number of changes in this curriculum. The Dearing Review (Dearing 1994) introduced a 'slimmed-down' version of the statutory curriculum, to be followed by a full-scale review in 2000. At the same time teachers in the primary sector are having to phase in a daily 'literacy hour' and 'numeracy hour'. Along with the curriculum changes, teachers are being expected to plan in a more structured and open way, which often involves planning with colleagues. Further, the introduction of regular, high-profile school inspections and the publication of performance tables have required teachers to produce a great deal more paper-based evidence. From this brief overview it is possible to see that the teacher may find it very difficult to give of their time freely to talk with a student when there are so many other demands being made upon them.

The curriculum followed by students in university education departments has changed considerably in the very recent past. This will be discussed further in the second section of the chapter. At this point it is worth noting that students have a 'packed' timetable in college and are required to carry out a comprehensive range of 'directed activities' while on placement. When analysing the data for this chapter there were a number of indications that teachers were unaware of, and wanted to be informed in detail about, the structure and content of the courses being followed by their student trainee.

Furthermore, many teachers appeared to be unaware of the wider pressures impacting upon student life. As one undergraduate commented, 'He didn't seem to understand that I had to leave early on Wednesdays so I could start my shift at work.' The funding arrangements for students mean that many have part-time jobs to support their studies, while some have care responsibilities at home.

These discussions serve to highlight the importance of the student making the class teacher aware of their own needs and at the same time seeking to establish a regular time for discussion. This needs to be carefully balanced so that the student does not appear to be drawing excessively upon the goodwill and time of the teacher.

The role of the school-based tutor

A number of university education departments have sought to establish partnerships with local schools so that the tutoring of students can be shared between college and school-based staff. This has now become a formal government requirement. As part of these initiatives, colleges are working with nominated members of school-based staff to teach, support and train students while on placement. Their roles vary, but typically they would embrace issues which relate to the school as a whole – examples, as illustrated in Goldsmiths partnership documentation, might include:

- negotiating placements of students within the school and liaison with the college;
- preparing the teaching and support staff in their role in supporting the students;
- liaison with parents and governors about the role of student teachers in the school;
- welcoming the students to the school and introducing them to the staff;
- providing practical details about the routines and policies of the school;
- providing a developmental programme of seminars on whole school issues;
- having an input into the college-based aspects of the students' courses, such as being involved in the planning and possibly the delivery of sessions.

In relation to individual students, the school-based tutor will have a central role in providing support and assessment. This will usually include:

- observation of taught sessions and monitoring of the student's file;
- written and verbal feedback about progress and the setting of targets for the student;
- liaison with the class teacher, college tutor and headteacher or head of department about the student's progress and issues that may arise;
- informal support and guidance about aspects of the student's role in school, providing a written report at the end of the student's placement;
- helping the student set targets for future development.

In terms of establishing and maintaining a professional working relationship with the school-based tutor, it is important that the student is aware of the way in which the role is viewed by the tutor themselves. Godley (cited in Kerry and Shelton Mayes 1995) identifies key areas where tutors perceive themselves as being more successful. These include being resource providers, evaluators and problem-solvers.

Analysis of quality assurance questionnaires indicates that the role is perceived and operated very differently from one school to another. In some schools, the time allocation for the school-based tutor to carry out their duties is tightly scheduled, and may involve them being released from teaching duties. In other schools, however, the approach may be more informal and flexible. It is important that the student clarifies when they are being formally assessed, otherwise, as one student commented: 'I wasn't sure if she was observing me as I relaxed in the staffroom with a coffee!'

It can be the case that the student seeks out the school-based tutor for practical advice and guidance about the day-to-day teaching in her or his classroom or lessons, when it would be more appropriate to ask the class teacher. The student may find it useful to establish when it is that the school-based tutor is available to talk with them and a scheduled regular time may reduce incidences of students overburdening the tutor with matters outside their domain.

The role of the college-based tutor/supervisor

As with the school-based tutor, the college-based tutor has responsibility to assess a student's progress and provide support, advice and guidance. They also have a key part to play in ensuring quality and equity across a range of students in a variety of contexts. Often they provide a vital channel of communication between college and school. The supervision of students, for some, will form part of a wider role as a lecturer in education, while for others they will focus on supporting students, and in some cases this will be for more than one university. It is important that students are aware of the constraints on the time of those coming into school to see them, and make every effort to be in a position where the tutor can observe them teach and talk with them. This is helped greatly if the student negotiates a time when the visit will take place, although events in the school or changes to the tutor's commitments may mean the plans have to alter at the last minute. This being the case, it is helpful if parties communicate the changes to each other. Feedback from school-based colleagues identifies both negotiation and communication as key factors in the success of partnerships with college.

Once again, the relationship will be more productive for all concerned if the student makes the tutor aware of aspects of their progress and issues that are concerning them, and actively seeks the advice that they feel they need. The resulting support and guidance can be more focused and purposeful.

Analysis of quality assurance data has highlighted a trend identified by a number of class teachers. They view their role in supporting students as being devalued by the emergence of the role of school-based tutor. One teacher commented: 'The college tutor seemed to bypass me and head for the school-based tutor. It was as if I had nothing important to say about the student.'

It is important that the college-based tutor gains a broad and objective view of the student's practice. In part this can be achieved by discussing the practice with a range of school-based colleagues, including the headteacher, student, class teacher and school-based tutor. As a third party, outside the school, it can often be easier for the college-based tutor to discuss sensitive and difficult issues that may arise. On this basis it may be appropriate for the student to consult the college tutor should they be unable to resolve issues that arise in school.

In gaining an overall perspective, the college-based tutor will be involved in many aspects of the student's practice and carry out a range of duties which mirror those discussed in relation to the school-based tutor.

The last three sections have highlighted and explored those individuals who our research suggests are most closely involved and influential in the student's work in school. To varying degrees, all, including the student, are involved in the assessment process. Fish's (1989) research highlights the pitfalls of the various adaptations of the 'apprenticeship model' of teacher education. She appeals to those involved in ITT to move forward by supporting a partnership model, where students, teachers and supervisors work together to reflect and develop each other's practice. From within this reflective framework valid judgements about student performance can be made. Students can contribute to this by initiating discussions about their practice and broadening the debate to consider, for example, national initiatives in education. They also have a responsibility to evaluate their placement through any formal channels that exist, such as quality assurance questionnaires.

The following sections identify and explore a range of individuals from the wider school community, who, while not necessarily closely involved in the work of the student, nevertheless have an impact upon their performance.

The role of the headteacher or senior manager

The role of the headteacher or head of department in relation to supporting students will vary greatly from school to school and depend upon their management style and philosophy. Some heads may introduce themselves and then remain in the background as far as the student is concerned, leaving the tutors and teachers to provide day-to-day support and guidance. Others, however, will make themselves available for discussion and offer advice as they see fit. It is important that the student is sensitive to the role that the head has adopted, but can initiate a discussion should they feel they need to. Informal discussions with primary student teachers highlight that heads are not always aware of what students are expected to do in school, and either expect too much of them or do not give them enough responsibility. It is up to the student to make their needs known, and where necessary to ask their tutor(s) to become involved.

Support staff

Students placed in a range of schools will soon come to appreciate that the numbers of, and duties undertaken by, support staff vary greatly from school to school. In general it could be said that the younger the children are, the more likely one is to see support staff working alongside the teacher in the classroom or withdrawing groups. Usually they are working under the guidance of the class teacher, who will be responsible for the overall management and learning that takes place in the room. Questionnaire data reveals that the following individuals are those that feature most often in student's work in schools. The commentary following each is an attempt to clarify and define the roles.

Nursery nurses

These staff usually work in nursery schools or early years classrooms. In the majority of cases they will have pursued an appropriate qualification related to the development, care and learning of pre-school and early years children. In many nursery classrooms they have an input into the planning of the curriculum, will initiate ideas and work with children involved in a range of activities. Students often comment that they find nursery nurses very supportive in providing practical help, although some students find it a challenge to establish an appropriate relationship. Part of a student teacher's development is learning to manage other adults in the class, who will be supporting the work they have planned. For many students, particularly those who have only recently completed their own schooling, it can prove quite daunting to manage an adult experienced in their own field. Class teachers and nursery nurses often build up very close, and sometimes intuitive working relationships. It may prove difficult for the student to enter into this already established working unit.

Classroom assistants

These members of staff will have a variety of roles, depending upon the school, and they may or may not have a formal qualification. In some cases they will withdraw groups to support particular curriculum areas, such as cooking or reading, or work alongside the teacher in the room. Some assistants will be employed to work with children who have specific learning difficulties. They will have an allotted time to work with the group or individual, depending upon circumstances. It is important that the student identifies how the class teacher works with the assistant, and should be prepared to plan for and brief them accordingly.

Technicians

Technicians are commonly found in secondary school departments, such as science, technology and art, where a good deal of practical work is undertaken by pupils as part of their normal lessons. They often have appropriate qualifications or life experience in the specialist activities which they prepare, assist and clear away. They order and store materials and equipment, carrying out routine maintenance. As above, it is important to observe how teachers negotiate technician assistance and to be sensitive to the level of support that can be expected.

Learning support teachers or other professional adults

Some children who have particular learning needs or medical conditions may have extra support provided by an appropriately qualified adult. It is often the case that they will plan a programme for the child and brief the class teacher. They will often withdraw the child for specialist support and also suggest how ongoing help can be provided in the classroom. It is important that the student seeks to draw upon the expertise of these specialists and acts upon advice given.

Volunteer helpers

A variety of members of the general public may seek to spend time as a volunteer helper in a school. They may be a parent, a member of the local community or those wishing to gain experience of working with children. They help in a variety of ways, such as supporting a reading group, helping with a craft activity or covering books and mounting displays. In establishing a positive working relationship, it is important that the student remains professional in their approach, ensuring they do not disclose inappropriate confidential information about the children or other staff. It is often a good idea to establish any areas of expertise the volunteer may have and plan activities that will draw upon these. It is important that the helper is carefully briefed so that they understand the aims of the activity they may be supporting.

The role of parents

Communication and contact arrangements between school and parents will vary from school to school, and it is important that the student works within any guidelines that are in place. The majority of parents are supportive of students on placement; however, they are naturally concerned about their child's education and well-being. Students need to communicate clearly and confidently with parents, but should they be approached about an issue they may be unsure of, they should seek the advice of the class teacher or head. Many students are required to be involved in parent consultations, but should the teacher or parent feel uneasy, the student should volunteer to withdraw.

Summary

Section 1 has highlighted and explored the roles of the key individuals with whom initial trainees are likely to have to establish positive working relationships. As indicated in the opening remarks, every student will be entering their 'training' with a unique range of life experiences and skills, but it is hoped that all can experience a little of what this final practice student enjoyed:

> I was able to ask the questions I needed to and I was given space to make some mistakes too. The best bit was discussing the children and the work at the end of the day. I think the teacher really valued my input.

Those returning to full- or part-time study

The second part of this chapter addresses issues relating to professional relationships from the perspective of those pursuing, and those working with students aiming for, an additional or higher qualification in education. As with those embarking on their initial qualification, there appear to be a range of reasons which influence the decision to pursue further study. Informal discussions with those returning to study indicate that the most common motivating factors are personal and career development. Students' personal and work circumstances will influence the path that they take in achieving their higher degree.

A theme which penetrates the following discussions relates to the status that the student is perceived as having and the way in which they plan and carry out their work in school. Further degree work is often research-based and involves the student observing and analysing practice in schools. Walford (1994) highlights that educational research has historically employed a methodology which involves 'researching down' and investigating those less powerful, often children and teachers. The analysis of the questionnaire data suggests that this is still the predominant model used by those following in-service or part-time degree courses. However, we noted a number of examples where students were simultaneously adopting a 'researching up' model, when they interviewed, for example, the headteacher, members of the Local Education Authority and governing bodies. These are factors which can significantly affect the success of the relationships formed.

This section of the chapter is subdivided to reflect the fact that many students choose to study on a part-time basis while they remain teaching in school, whereas others find it suits their circumstances to become a full-time student once again. I begin by exploring issues of relevance to those in part-time study, and then forcus on the full-time student. When the questionnaire data was analysed it appeared that the issues in relation to the college tutor, external agencies and parents were similar regardless of the type of course being followed, and therefore I conclude by covering areas of relevance to both groups.

Those returning to part-time study

The role of the student

There are many teachers who choose to pursue an additional or higher qualification while they remain in full-time employment. These students are often working towards a certificate, diploma or master's degree. This section is particularly concerned with those students who, as part of their qualification, are required to research some aspect of education within their own school. They may be motivated by one or a number of factors, which include:

- personal career or professional development;
- personal interest in an aspect of education;
- a need identified within the school.

The questionnaire responses suggest there is a range of areas of interest that students research in their own schools. These can be grouped together to include one or more of the following:

- pedagogical issues relating to specific curriculum areas or aspects of classroom practice;
- explorations into the role of whole school management and organisation systems;
- the analysis and application of central legislation and national policies;
- theories relating to resourcing, managing and co-ordinating a curriculum area or subject department.

Reflecting upon how they approach research is a central responsibility for all students, but there are particular issues which are unique to students researching in their own place of work. Within the context of this chapter it is appropriate to explore some of the factors which affect the working relationships.

Students need to be aware of their dual role within the school. On the one hand they are viewed by staff as colleagues with whom they need to maintain a positive working relationship long after the research is completed. In contrast, they may be adopting a critically reflective approach to their own practice and often that of their colleagues. The student needs to consider whether they are conveying a 'researching down' attitude and approach or whether they are emphasising the equality in the relationship with the researched colleagues. This may be easier to reflect if the student is a participant observer (see Chapter 9). Even more conducive to positive relationships may be to try to 'research up' when working with colleagues and draw upon their expertise which you may not have. Above all, it is important that the student makes it a priority to identify any sensitivities or areas in which colleagues may feel vulnerable, and to use this information to inform the methods employed. The impetus behind a student carrying out a research project can often be to change an aspect of practice within the school. If this is the case, it is important that the student liaises with colleagues and provides appropriate and sensitive feedback, while at the same time contextualising their work within the needs of the school. Maintaining confidentiality is of uppermost priority, whether it be with reference to samples of children's work or discussing a colleague's practice. Further, it is important that the student demonstrates to all who are being asked to give support that they themselves are committed to what they are studying and are giving freely of their own time.

The role of colleagues

The role of colleagues in supporting in-service study will vary greatly according to the nature of the research project being undertaken. Generally, however, they may be involved in one or more of the following:

- providing data by answering questionnaires, being interviewed and observed at work;
- trialling materials and ideas within their own taught sessions and feeding back the data;
- discussing evidence gathered and providing an insight into the accuracy of results collected from groups they may teach;
- acting as a 'critical friend' with whom the student can discuss their ideas.

In order to maintain a positive working relationship with colleagues it is important that the student takes the initiative. Discussions with selected questionnaire respondents identified the following as practical suggestions for maintaining positive relationships with colleagues:

- Seek to clarify the objectives of the project – this may involve frequent informal discussions and/or structured staff meeting time. Colleagues may be reassured if they meet with college tutors and/or senior members of the school staff who can be asked to demonstrate their commitment to the project.
- Provide regular informal and formal feedback as to the progress of the work. This could vary from 'chatting' with a colleague to providing interim written reports. It may also be appropriate to set aside a regular time when colleagues can approach the student with issues.
- Provide opportunities for interested colleagues to become involved in the work. This may be through discussing ideas, reading draft reports, volunteering to trial materials or strategies with their own classes or having their practice analysed.
- Respect colleagues' privacy by ensuring confidentiality is maintained.
- Adopt an open and enquiring approach, avoiding situations whereby the student is appearing to pass judgement on the ideas and practices of their colleagues.

The role of the headteacher/senior manager

The role of the headteacher or senior manager can vary, from themselves as the student, pursuing an in-service course, to someone who is the subject of research. If the headteacher takes the role of a student exploring practice in their own school, then they will almost always be adopting methods which necessarily appear to be 'researching down', since they are the most senior member of staff within the research field. If you are a headteacher it is imperative that you are aware of this and approach the research in a manner which identifies clear aims and objectives, and makes clear to staff an identified time when you are 'researching' rather than fulfilling one of your other roles as head. This is particularly the case if, for example, the focus of the project is upon sensitive issues. One headteacher who responded to our questionnaire commented that they felt it more appropriate to explore the effects of teacher appraisal on professional development in a school other than their own.

In terms of supporting staff researching within their school, a headteacher or senior manager can provide support for them in a number of ways. These may include one or more of the following:

- providing opportunities to discuss their progress and providing a broader perspective on the issues the student may be researching;
- helping to identify the school's needs which may be supported by their research;
- lending support by providing resources, release time, study leave and possibly funding for their course;
- 'publicising' their support for the project by discussing it with staff and parents and, where appropriate, placing it on the school/department's development plan;
- providing data to support the project.

In order to receive continuing support from the head/senior manager and to maintain a positive working relationship, it is important that the student, where relevant:

- demonstrates their commitment by attending college-based sessions and managing their increased workload, maintaining their 'normal' duties within the school to the best of their ability;
- provides verbal or written feedback on the progress of the project;
- maintains the confidentiality of discussions with the head/senior manager, particularly when the student may be discussing the practice of colleagues;
- relates the findings of the research to the needs of the school, and where possible provides practical suggestions for colleagues and redrafts policies.

Our questionnaire data suggests that students were more likely to maintain positive working relationships with senior managers when they managed to combine their own needs with those of the school, and where they made a conscious decision to be explicit and forthcoming about their progress. Ultimately it is the head's responsibility to ensure the quality of education in their school, and where they can see the student's work contributing to this they are more likely to be accommodating, interested, supportive and flexible.

Those returning to full-time study

The role of the student

This section sets out to explore those issues which will be of unique relevance to those who already have an initial teaching qualification and decide to take time out of work to pursue an additional or higher qualification. In some cases the student may be taking a sabbatical period of study, and others may choose to study in another country. In the majority of cases, where they are required to work within schools, they will be having to establish relationships with institutions that are new to them. Some students' research will necessitate them visiting a range of schools to gather data to contrast, while others will wish to base themselves in one school. In all cases it is important for good relationships if the student considers:

- the research methods adopted. Although the students may not perceive it themselves, many teachers in schools will perceive them as 'researching down' and to ensure teachers are willing to participate and provide accurate data, it is important that the student avoids situations in which the teachers feel vulnerable and under threat;
- whether they are sufficiently familiar with the educational system in which they are going to be working. This may require some background reading relating to legislation, policy and practice;
- how they can make their research objectives very clear, providing opportunities for the staff, managers and parents to clarify how the data they provide will be used and confidentiality maintained;
- how they can provide regular feedback on the findings as the work proceeds and report at the end of the project;
- how they can demonstrate, at appropriate times, how much they value the support of the school. This may be through discussing their work with staff and asking for feedback, or officially acknowledging them in the final report.

The role of the class teacher

The role of the class teacher will vary according to the focus of the research. If the research student is exploring curriculum issues they may be providing the means for the student to do their work, for example by providing access to a group of children with whom they can work. However, they may also be the subject of the research for reasons to do with pedagogy. In either situation it is important that the student draws upon the expertise of the teacher and discusses their work with the teacher, thus giving some sense of ownership and involvement in the work. A student may call upon the class teacher to be involved in one or more of the following:

- answering questionnaires, being involved in interviews and providing data;
- allowing the student to observe and discuss their practice;
- providing access to a group of children so that the student can observe them working, talking to or interviewing them, and sometimes acting as a participant observer trialling ideas with the children;

- discussing the work of the children to validate and assess their performance in trials or observations.

It can be daunting for the student, working in a strange and unfamiliar environment among people they do not know. Questionnaire responses would suggest that the relationships established are more positive and mutually productive if the student takes every opportunity to discuss their work with the class teacher. One student highlights this when she comments that 'I felt really out of place at times, was given my group for an allotted time each week and there was no communication between myself and the class teacher. With hindsight I would have welcomed the chance to discuss the work with her.'

The role of the headteacher/senior manager

As a full-time student researching in a school, it is possible to spend extensive periods of time observing or carrying out other forms of research. During these periods the head is, in effect, acting as a host and will have to justify your presence.

If the research is of benefit to the school, then it is the role of the head to support that research and the researcher as much as possible. The student may wish to consider the following as strategies for establishing and maintaining positive working relationships with headteachers:

- providing a written outline of the intended project and the aims of the research, including some background and context for the work;
- providing some indication of how the project may benefit the school;
- providing regular feedback as to the progress of the project and disseminating the results through a written report, presentation to the staff, governors and possibly parents;
- indicating how they can be flexible in their approach so as to reflect the needs and circumstances of the school or department in which they are working.

The student may also wish to ask the head for statistical data about, for example, performance in subject areas or National Curriculum tests. On the other hand they may wish to gather subjective, qualitative information about teaching methodologies and staff attitudes. In both cases the information is often confidential and the head must be reassured that the data is going to be used anonymously and sensitively, and not in a way that will damage the school or its staff. Offering to provide a draft report may serve to alleviate these worries.

Common issues and relationships

The following paragraphs explore common issues and relationships for postgraduate students, whether they be full-time or in-service. It is interesting to note that it is the relationships within the wider community, and outside the classroom, which the two groups perceive as posing similar issues for them as students.

The role of the college tutor

Students working towards an additional or higher qualification in education differ from initial teacher trainees in that it is not usual for the college tutor to assess their practice and competence as a teacher. Although tutors are responsible for assessing the student, it is usually the written presentation of their ideas that forms the basis of the assessment. It is also unusual for the assessments to involve any teacher-colleagues based in school. However, the student's presence in school may have implications for a school-based tutor if the college tutors suggest they pursue a particular issue or aspect of work within the school context.

In addition to working in the school setting, the student's relationships with the college-based tutor will encompass the range of activities typical of a college setting, such as acquaintance with theory; focusing thinking and providing a context for work. This relationship will stand alongside relations as experienced in the school context and requires sensitivity and flexibility from the student as they move between the two. One student who returned the questionnaire commented that the most positive aspect of the working relationship with her tutor was the fact that he gave her the self-confidence to complete a complex research project which involved translating theory into practice in a busy school environment. As she said, 'He made me believe I could do it!'

During the initial stages of a working relationship with a tutor, a student may feel uneasy about working with someone who may be an expert in their field. It is imperative that the student approaches this situation in a positive frame of mind, realising how much they can benefit from the relationship. It is helpful if the student is pro-active and asks informed questions. This necessarily implies that they must be prepared for their tutorial, having read relevant material and completed any agreed work. The initiative to arrange meetings, set targets and complete drafts of reports must be taken by the student themselves. It is important, however, that the tutor's dual roles are not compromised. The tutor is both a supporter and a critical friend, as well as an assessor who will judge any pieces of submitted work. In order to maintain the distinction it is imperative that the student respects the tutor's roles by not requesting inappropriate guidance. There may be times, for example, when comments in detail about phrasing used in a draft report would be less helpful than comments which focused upon the main ideas.

The role of external agencies

As part of their research, many students may seek the involvement of external agencies. These may be groups of experts which provide support or work with schools, such as the social services or the Local Education Authority. However, students may also wish to work with agencies who, historically, have no links with school. One student who responded to the questionnaire identified how he had established a relationship with a theatre group in order to research and develop the teaching of design and technology in his primary school. Other groups may include religious communities or local industry. The issues relating to different agencies may be quite distinct.

Organisations which provide support or work alongside schools will have some knowledge of the working environment to which the research may relate. It is also true to say that many of these organisations, such as the police, social services, medical practitioners, school psychological services and LEAs, are often dealing with confidential and sensitive information. In order to maintain good relationships it is incumbent upon the student to ensure that confidentiality will be respected.

Organisations such as local industries and religious communities are often very keen to establish links with their local schools for a number of reasons; often it may be that they wish to be known and accepted within the area. It may also form part of their mission to support and give something back to the local population. Students approaching such groups need to be aware that such 'agendas' may be operating and that they will be working with people who are unlikely to be trained to work with children. It is the student's responsibility to make their research aims as clear as possible and provide feedback to the groups who have provided support. In replying to our questionnaire, the student mentioned above, pursuing an in-service course, commented on how much a theatre group had been prepared to contribute to the technology project he was researching. One frustration had been that other school colleagues were not as committed as he was, therefore not providing a consistent response when working with the theatre company.

The role of parents

Many parents appreciate the need for educational research and are willing to be supportive of projects being carried out which involve their children. Naturally, however, the principal concern is for the education of their child, and students should be aware that they need to reassure parents that the work will in no way jeopardise the child's progress. Informal feedback from teachers and personal experience have highlighted a range of strategies that can assist working relationships with parents. These include:

- highlighting the potential benefits for the child;
- seeking parents' permission to involve their child, through writing directly to them or using the usual channels of communication available in the school;
- ensuring confidentiality and anonymity;
- reflecting upon their research methods so that no group or child can appear to be deliberately placed in a position where they are receiving an inferior input or experience for the purposes of comparison;
- providing an opportunity for parents to be able to discuss their concerns with the student, either individually or through a group meeting.

It may be the case that, where a student is researching in the school where they also teach, parents will need reassurance that they can fulfil the dual role without compromising their child's education. Many parents would welcome it if the student were to take the time to explain how their research was feeding directly into policy and practice in the school and therefore having a direct benefit on their child's education.

Concluding comments

This chapter has set out to explore and highlight some of the factors that will be influential in shaping the success of the relationships established while education students are working in schools. A number of underlying and unifying threads can be traced throughout the issues relating to both initial trainees and those returning to study. These can be translated into a set of principles which, if adhered to, should significantly enhance the success of the professional working relationships established during all courses of study. These principles include:

- keeping in mind the other person's point of view;
- reflecting upon the manner in which you and your work are perceived by those you relate to;
- where appropriate, being open and explicit about your work, making your needs and findings clear; and
- being pro-active, wherever possible seeking to take the initiative.

At the heart of this discussion is the view that education takes place within communities of people, whether these be schools or colleges. Communities thrive and prosper on the vitality brought by individuals working together. This involves reflection and discussion, and if these are abundant then the student and all those they are working with will have their ideas challenged, their thinking developed, and consequently their practice enhanced.

References

Dearing, R. (1994) *The National Curriculum and its Assessment: Final Report,* London: SCAA.

Fish, D. (1989) *Learning Through Practice in Initial Teacher Training,* London: Kogan Page.

Kendall, S., Allebone, B. and Griffiths, J. (1997) 'Different voices in partnership', *Mentoring and Tutoring* 5, 2: 39–44.

Kerry, T. and Shelton Mayes, A. (eds) (1995) *Issues in Mentoring,* London: Routledge.

Walford, G. (ed.) (1994) *Researching the Powerful in Education,* London: UCL Press.

Whitty, G. (1995) 'Quality control in teacher education', in T. Kerry and A. Shelton Mayes (eds) *Issues in Mentoring,* London: Routledge.

11 Some final comments

John Jessel

In this book we have considered some general aspects of study, such as how you can approach and monitor your learning and how you may function as a person in terms of managing the pressures of time and other demands. We have also looked at the ways that you can work with a variety of media in order to obtain information and to develop and present your ideas. Also, at a more general level, we have outlined some approaches where study involves moving beyond published works and is to do with finding things out through, for example, dealing directly with people and events. However, in relation to teaching and education, there are particular issues concerning the scope of a course of study, and to this end we have included chapters which consider such factors as the different historical, social and political forces that can come into play through the development or imposition of a curriculum, and how these can affect teaching and learning. We have also looked at how the notion of a curriculum has been studied, and have argued that, as teachers, we may also need to develop an awareness of how knowledge and understandings can be categorised, how different subjects, or areas of content, have evolved and the demands that can be made upon learners. Finally, if you are studying to teach then you may also be concerned with your own role as a professional, the roles of others, and how you relate to a variety of people in a variety of settings. Being highly proficient with regard to any one or two of the above aspects of study may be relatively easy. Ensuring that you do not neglect the other aspects, however, can be very demanding as you seek to find a balance among the different areas and the demands that they entail. By providing an overview, we hope that this book will assist in getting a balance in approaches so that one aspect of study supports another.

As part of the reflective process it is natural to reappraise the purpose of study. What you gain can have as many dimensions as the process of study itself. Formal assessments which can lead to academic or vocational awards are likely to feature among the short-term goals. In the long term, much of what you gain may be unspoken and form part of your own personal development and the ability to be instrumental in the development of others. In the short term, you may be assessed in ways which range from observing your skills in the classroom to allowing you the opportunity to demonstrate your ability to express an argument in writing, either in an examination or as a longer essay or dissertation. While you are engaged in a course of study, short-term hurdles can loom large and so it is worth focusing on these for a moment. Although the possibility for self-assessment is widely acknowledged, assessment invariably involves a summary of your abilities that is made by other people. As such, your perceptions of the way others see you can become a major issue and lead to distortions in what you do. Written essays or answers to examination questions can provide an example of this. Although these can provide an opportunity for the ideal student to display their understanding and command of an area, many of us do not fit into the category of 'ideal student'. Instead, we can fall into the trap of adopting strategies which give the impression that learning has taken place. This can result in an emphasis on memorising rather than understanding (Boud 1990).

There can also be a mismatch between students' perceptions of the criteria used for marking their essays and the actual criteria that tutors said they used. For example, Norton (1990) has found that students expressed a belief that tutors look for content and knowledge, while tutors said that the key factor was how students form an argument in order to address a question. The possibility that in practice tutors may operate a different set of marking criteria, such as expecting to see a particular viewpoint put forward in an essay, has also been investigated by Norton *et al.* (1996). They found that students from different courses and different colleges not only held but also acted upon the widespread belief that credit would result from a whole range of tactics not related to the kind of learning likely to lead to depth of understanding. Such tactics included using big words or technical terms to impress, reflecting the tutor's opinions as closely as possible, choosing the easiest title, and making the text visually exciting by using fancy designs for headings. Although it was held that such tactics were not explicitly encouraged by tutors, the extent to which students could, wittingly or unwittingly, be rewarded for such tactics still needs to be researched. In view of the above issues, it may help to find opportunities for discussion with tutors on a regular basis, and to find ways of expressing and sharing ideas on what is expected at different stages of a course and for different assignments. In any event, it is important that you are clear about the purpose of an assignment, look carefully at any assessment criteria and, if necessary, discuss what they mean and find out whether some carry more weight than others.

What you gain from study in the long term may emerge in the way you see yourself rather than in the way others see you. For example, one commonly noticed effect of studying is that as you try to find out more you are also likely to discover that in turn there is more to be found out. Knowing that there is more to be found out can have an effect upon your involvement and interest in an area.

You may also find that the way that you approach study can have more to do with the process of asking questions and becoming involved than the area or topic that you are studying. People have differing views on whether a given topic is interesting or uninteresting. In turn, this suggests that the latter qualities may not be intrinsic to the topic; they are more to do with the person concerned. Through your approach to study you have the opportunity to make a topic interesting – or otherwise. This may be a factor to bear in mind in those moments when you find it difficult trying to decide what to study. Although there may be an element of risk and uncertainty in whatever area you choose, we hope that you will find a way to make your discoveries enjoyable.

References

Boud, D. (1990) 'Assessment and the promotion of academic values', *Studies in Higher Education* 15, 1: 101–11.

Norton, L.S. (1990) 'Essay-writing: what really counts?', *Higher Education* 20: 411–42.

Norton, L., Dickins, T. and McLaughlin Cook, N. (1996) 'Coursework assessment: what are tutors really looking for?' in G. Gibbs (ed.) *Improving Student Learning*, Oxford: The Oxford Centre for Staff Development.

Index of Names

Index of Subjects